BRITISH TEETH

BRITISH TEETH

WILLIAM LEITH

Illustrations by Michael Heath

 SHORT BOOKS

FRONT LINES

First published in 2001 by
Short Books
15 Highbury Terrace
London N5 1UP

A CIP catalogue record for this book
is available from the British Library.

ISBN 0 571 20865 7

Printed in Great Britain by
Bookmarque Ltd, Croydon, Surrey

To Lotta and 'Mr Dog'

WHEN THE TOOTH went, when it finally snapped, we were sitting in a café in the middle of London. I remember the name of the café, the street, the district, the postal code, and the widely used nickname for the general area, but I hesitate, for the moment, to use these names. I was in a 200-year-old building, in a street of 200-year-old buildings leaning against each other. I was having a conversation about the decline of British storytelling – the fact that we, the British, were finding it hard to write novels and make films about ourselves.

It was a spring day in 1995. We had won the war, and lost our empire, and I was about to bite into a ciabatta sandwich with salad and mozzarella cheese. The tooth was throbbing, but not unpleasantly. My girlfriend was sitting opposite me. The café, being British, was slightly embarrassing. Our table was made of Formica, an attempt to make the place look down in the mouth, like an old-fashioned greasy spoon, and therefore, in an ironic way, classy. It was trying hard to look as if it was not trying hard. The prices were restaurant prices. We were fools.

We had just watched a film, Robert Redford's *Quiz Show*, starring the British actor Ralph Fiennes. The day before, we had seen Oliver Stone's *Natural Born Killers*. The killers, played by Woody Harrelson and Juliette Lewis, had raged around America exuberantly, cinematically. It had made me think about British killers, how small-time and seedy they seemed in comparison, how they tended to do their killing quietly, without charisma, in festering Victorian houses. Dennis Nilsen, Fred West, Reginald Christie, Dr Crippen. Hardly Ted Bundy, the much-fancied killer who looked like Warren Beatty, or Clyde Barrow, who was played by Warren Beatty. Hardly O.J. Simpson, with his false beard and his Ford Bronco, with his huge, magnetic smile, his gated residence, his mysterious movements in the car park on the night of the killing.

I was full of the intensity of a man who has just come out of the cinema. I had the sandwich in my right hand. My fingers were dusted with flour. *Quiz Show* is a film based on a true story about the rigging of an American television show. Described like this, it sounds dull. In fact, it's so good that it makes you believe, for a while, that this small misdemeanour was just about the most important thing that ever happened. For two hours, you think: Alexander the Great, William the Conqueror, the Second World War, and the rigging of this show, *Twenty-One*. It seems to be telling you the history of America in a thimble. It's about Jews, WASPs, snobbery, accent and class. When I came out of the cinema, I was thinking: if the British made a film like this, it would fail at every level. We wouldn't get it right. In fact, we wouldn't want to get it right. That's the main point. It would involve more introspection than we could bear.

The sandwich was two inches from my mouth. I was already processing, on a subconscious level, the infor-mation I needed to guide it into the right, non-throbbing side of my mouth. I had reached the stage of not wanting to risk the left side. Dentally speaking, I was incisive, but barely masticatory. But I had been coping with this new incapacity for months. I was fine. Sometimes I felt nauseous and feverish, and I was beginning to wonder if this was in some way connected to the tooth. But I had become good at putting these suspicions out of my mind. I lowered the sandwich an inch, and said, 'We can't tell stories about ourselves any more.'

My girlfriend said, 'What?'

Nobody believes you at first, when you say this. A nation which has lost the ability to tell stories? It does not seem likely, or even possible.

I said, 'The art of British storytelling has degenerated. We've forgotten how to do it.'

My girlfriend said, 'What are you saying?'

What *was* I saying? It was something that had been nagging away at me for a while. Naturally, part of me didn't want to believe it either. Perhaps it wasn't true. Perhaps I was neurotic, or having some sort of crisis of my own. I kept looking at the places around me. Buildings and streets, whole towns and cities even, seemed insubstantial. They seemed to have been leached of meaning. Even the names sounded wrong. The names didn't have a ring to them. They had, in some complicated, embarrassing way, lost their dignity.

Take the word 'British'. What would you mean if you said that something was 'very British'?

You would mean that the thing is old, crumbling, declined, corrupt. As an idea, it is almost the same as 'English', but not exactly; it has a ring of acquisition, imperialism. The word is a reminder of ancient sins. It can no longer be used in its old sense, to mean tolerant, fair-minded, self-sacrificing, incorruptible, amateur in the best way, gentlemanly, stoical and decent. You can't say 'That's not very British of you, old boy' and expect any sympathy.

These days, we have a suspicion that the people who originally used the expression were themselves not particularly tolerant, fair-minded, self-sacrificing or gentlemanly; in the popular imagination, they went around brutalising foreigners, in order to make them go to church and drink tea and eat sponge cake. Which may not have been far from the truth.

British – the word has lost its ring. It was, of course, absolutely fine to call a book *American Psycho*. But 'British Psycho'? 'British Psycho' sounds unappealing, to say the least. As do 'British Beauty', 'British Pie', 'Young Brits', 'British Tabloid', 'British Tragedy', 'How to Make a British Quilt'. And what about 'Last Exit to Hackney'? Or 'Fear and Loathing in Blackpool'? Or 'A Year in Sussex'? British names have become worn-out. Something about them – their ability to serve as the backdrops for interesting stories – has decayed over time. I once read a magazine questionnaire in which someone, a woman, was asked where was the strangest place she had had sex. The idea was to say something like 'at the cinema', or 'in the airing cupboard'. The woman's answer was 'Hull'. And the reason this was funny was the name 'Hull' – the weariness of it, its connotations of dullness and destitution. Hull does sound like a strange place to have sex.

I'd been reading American novels, particularly the beginnings of American novels, and finding myself freshly surprised and envious each time some author had casually, unself-consciously mentioned the names of cities and streets and areas. They were always heading up Lexington and going down Broadway, hanging out in the Village, cruising along Sunset to the beach. British geography was not the same. One diminished oneself, for instance, by walking along Hampstead High Street, or Trumpington Road. You could not begin a novel by saying, 'I walked down Hampstead High Street, towards Haverstock Hill.' Or 'I walked along Trumpington Road, towards King's Parade.' Or the ghastly: 'I walked along the High, and turned into the Turl.' And this applied to conversation as well. Even in conversation you had to be careful about the names you used. You could not say, 'Anyway, there I was, in Mayfair...' without laying yourself open to ridicule.

In fact, I'd been in this exact situation recently. Something had happened to me in Mayfair. I'd run into an old friend. A day later, I was sitting at a table, with several people, and I told them about it. I said, 'I ran into Jim.'

'Where?'

Where? I hesitated. The answer was 'in Mayfair'. But I could not say 'in Mayfair'. You don't say 'in Mayfair'. It's just not done. I hesitated. Should I say, 'the West End?' This would be geographically accurate, but slightly misleading. People would think I meant Soho, or Covent Garden.

I said, 'Just around... Old Bond Street.' I blushed. It still sounded like an embarrassing place to be. But Mayfair! 'Mayfair' would have been disastrous. Somebody would have raised their eyebrows and said, 'Ooh!'

As a place name, Mayfair had degenerated so badly that it could no longer be used.

On a train ride a few days before, I'd sat behind a British man and an American woman who were getting to know each other. She was from Baltimore and he was from Leeds. I couldn't see them, but I could hear their conversation. They were flirting. They would, I thought, end up in bed together that night for the first time. He asked her what Baltimore was like. She said, 'Well...' And then she told him – the ethnic make-up of the population, the size of the city in relation to other American cities, how Baltimore was viewed from the outside, how its own citizens viewed it. She talked about weather conditions. She mentioned Barry Levinson, who was from Baltimore, and whose film *Diner* was set in Baltimore.

Diner! A film about ordinary, middle-class people, people who are witty and exuberant, but also vulnerable. People who had been defined by growing up in Baltimore, but by no means smothered. They existed as individuals. In Baltimore! Britain's equivalent city would be – what? Derby? Bolton? I can't see a version of *Diner* set in Derby or Bolton, featuring regular, middle-class people who live in nice houses but who are also sympathetic characters. It does not seem narratively possible.

And then the woman on the train said, 'What about Leeds? What's Leeds like?'

There was a silence. The man from Leeds was thinking. I knew exactly how he felt. I sympathised with his awkwardness. Leeds was one of the largest cities in Britain. Leeds was Britain's equivalent of, say, Boston or Detroit. But what the woman can't have understood is that when you grow up in Britain, you're not supposed to talk in detail about your home town. Things such as the population of the city, the way people in other cities see it, its notable institutions and famous inhabitants, are things one is supposed, in some elaborate, highly evolved way, to pretend not to know. You're supposed to go around not being bothered by these things, and never mentioning them.

The man from Leeds said, 'Dunno, really.' This is what he said about the huge, throbbing city which had moulded him. Mills, warehouses, steep redbrick terraces with views of hills, a burgeoning post-industrial economy, shopping malls, the recently opened Harvey Nichols department store. And what about the Leeds United of the early 1970s? Sprake, Reaney, Cooper, Bremner, Charlton, Hunter, Lorimer, Giles, Jones, Clarke, Gray. The instigation of a cynical, modern way of playing. The loss of the 1970 Cup Final by a whisker. The tragic death, from a wasting disease, of the controversial coach Don Revie, who had gone on to manage the England team. I had only ever been to Leeds a handful of times. This guy had grown up there, and all he had to say was, 'Dunno, really.' He said it in a murky Leeds accent: 'Dernerr, ruhrly.'

But, as I say, I could understand this. I would probably have done the same.

It occurred to me that perhaps we, as Brits, are suffering from something like a superiority complex. By this, I don't mean that we are superior. To have a superiority complex, you don't actually have to be superior, or even to believe you're superior. The complex exists a long time after you have any claim to being superior, after others have stopped believing you to be superior, after it is generally accepted, in fact, that you are not necessarily superior to anybody. In racial terms, white people have a superiority complex. In sexual terms, it's heterosexuals. Between men and women, it's men.

Acceptable behaviour, as a British or white person, is not to draw attention to yourself, because if you draw attention to yourself, to your defining characteristics, you might offend people. You might be proud to be white, and not have a racist bone in your body, but you know not to draw attention to your racial pride. You're not supposed to talk about, or even to know, what it means to be white. It is something you must not be interested in. You can't say, of the Smiths, that they represent 'white music at its best'. You can say, 'I like black music', but you can't say, 'I like white music'. When Norman Mailer wrote about boxing, he wrote about white fighters and Black fighters. Black is a nomenclature; for the sake of tact, white must merely be a description. And if the Irish, as is sometimes said, are the blacks of Europe, then the British are the whites.

One's Britishness, then, like one's whiteness, is something awkward and difficult, something that must be handled with tact and discretion, and preferably hidden or masked. As a Brit, you worry that, if you're not careful, the slumbering dragon of intolerant behaviour might be awakened. You think of mass slaughter and slavery. You think of an empire built on sugar plantations in places such as Jamaica. As a Britisher, you do not, like the Irish and the Italians and the Belgians, smile and hoot the horn on your car and wave your national flag. You purse your lips, and keep your teeth covered. You drive along quietly, looking at the road. If you're tactful, you never even buy the flag.

I was once walking, with a woman, past a shop that sold neon light displays, and we stopped and looked in the window. On the far wall was a neon slogan, lit up, which said, 'None of us are Gods, but to be British is to walk in the shadow of God.'

The woman I was with said, 'That's appalling.'

I looked at the display. I didn't quite feel appalled. But I definitely felt uncomfortable. I asked her why she felt like she did.

'What do you mean? It's disgusting. Look at it!'

I said, 'Try substituting another country's name. Try "French".'

'French is not so bad. Still bad, but not so bad.'

'Belgian?'

'Fine.'

'Danish?'

'Perfect.'

'American?'

'You could make a case for it. "American" sounds more inclusive. It sounds like you're including blacks and Hispanics and so on.'

I said, 'I'm British and proud of it.' Then I gave her a funny look to show I was joking. She gave me a playful cuff. A moment of Brit-panic. Afterwards, we had a session of Brit-exorcism, telling each other hideous things about the British. I remembered a drama series which depicted a Brit going to live abroad. Referred to as a foreigner, he said, 'But I'm not foreign. I'm British!' After a while, we felt better.

***

When the tooth went, when it finally snapped, I was sitting in a café in Greek Street, in Soho, in the 'West End' of London, London W1, at around mid-day. A light rain had fallen, but the sky was bright. On the way to the café, we had been enthusing about Ralph Fiennes. For some reason, we knew that he had grown up in a Victorian mansion block in Clapham. Somebody had told me a story, possibly true, about borrowing a cup of sugar from Fiennes's father. Or was it that Fiennes's father had asked to borrow the cup of sugar? Another thing: one of Fiennes's bottom teeth was slightly out of alignment, and this seemed to give him an air of individuality, of quality. He had not compromised. He had not been bought. He

Ralph Fiennes

would not make dumb blockbuster movies, because he did not have dumb blockbuster teeth.

Looking for a place to have lunch, we had walked through the narrow streets of Soho, with their cracked 200-year-old buildings. We went past the house of the essayist William Hazlitt, who wrote, 'I have more confidence in the dead than the living.' Hazlitt himself had been dead for well over a century. We were in a literary necropolis. I remembered a story by John Updike, written in the 1960s, in which Updike, writing in the first person, described the reactions of an American character as he walked through the streets of London. 'The city', wrote Updike, 'overwhelmed our expectations. The Kiplingesque grandeur of Waterloo Station, the Eliotic despondency of the brick row in Chelsea where we spent the night in the flat of a vague friend, the Dickensian nightmare of fog and sweating pavement... all this seemed too authentic to be real, too corroborative of literature to be solid.'

Later, in a taxi, the Updike narrator says, 'We wheeled past mansions by Galsworthy and parks by A. A. Milne; we glimpsed a cobbled 18th-century alley, complete with hanging tavern boards, where Dr Johnson might have reeled and gasped the night he laughed so hard – the incident in Boswell so beautifully amplified in the essay by Beerbohm.'

When I saw this, I thought: what does this say about an

American's-eye view of London? That nothing written about London after the 1920s had successfully stamped itself on the American imagination? That 18th- and 19th-century descriptions were so vivid that they're impossible to forget? And what about that 'too corroborative of literature to be solid'? Here, Updike is telling us about a place which, 100 years ago, had been turned into a myth, a city which had, as the fulcrum of an empire, emanated literary importance. This place was the centre of the world. Naturally, it made a perfect backdrop for stories.

But somewhere between then and now, Britain had faded out of the literary landscape. We had been relegated from the first division! Surely this could not have happened without anybody noticing. None of my teachers at school, for instance, had told me about it. But it was true. Was this the reason a British *Quiz Show* would not have worked – that we, as a people, no longer felt important enough to bear any self-examination? Frankly, yes. We were, in some terrible sense, fatally embarrassed about the things which made us British. We were ashamed of what we had been and what we had become. We were in the insupportable position, not only of not being important enough, but also of not being unimportant enough. We were not a plucky little Belgium or Turkey or Liechtenstein, the sort of little tyke who might have great fun telling stories about himself. No, we were caught in a place of untold awkwardness – the recently ruined gentleman at the wedding, the former tyrant or martinet brought low. Something had gone terribly wrong, certainly, and it was still too soon to comfortably talk about it.

My girlfriend and I had glanced at French restaurants, Thai restaurants, a Hungarian restaurant. But we just wanted somewhere to have lunch, rather than some kind of international food event. We finally stopped outside the place with the Formica tables and took in the atmosphere: no meat, wholefood, vaguely counter-cultural. It was pretentious but unfussy. It contained irony.

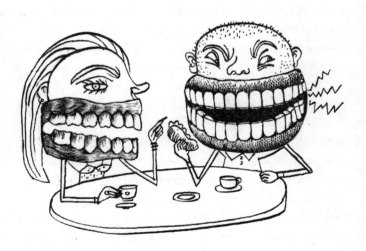

It was the best that we could do. Inside, we ordered our ciabatta sandwiches – an obscure homage to the Mediterranean, to olive oil and fatty cheese, to the sun, to a level of authenticity which was, we must have felt, somehow missing from our lives. When he is abroad, an Italian or a Frenchman, or a Japanese, seeks out his own food. But we, middle-class Brits, don't even want ours when we're at home. We all know that an educated Briton is a man who has formed his tastes by looking outside Britain, to places where things are genuine, rather than themed, where traditions are upheld proudly, rather than by bigots and philistines. French bread, French wine, Italian bread, Italian coffee.

I said, 'Cappuccino, please.'

I didn't order tea. Tea seems dull. When Boy George said that he would 'rather have a cup of tea' than have sex, he was saying, 'I'd rather do something dull than have sex.' He would not have been making quite the same point if he'd said, 'I'd rather have an espresso', even if he'd been Italian. The Italians do not associate their national drink with dullness. But neither did we, 100 years ago. When people are going around the world, slaughtering foreigners in their thousands in order to make British customs the blueprint for the world, these customs do not seem dull.

Far from it – they seem fascinating. Invading and subduing more than a quarter of the world must have given the cup of tea, as a punctuation point in the day, a real edge. When, in *Barchester Towers*, Anthony Trollope wrote pages of stuff about people agonising over how to separate the posh people from the slightly less posh people at a tea party, it did not seem fey and trivial. He wrote it with conviction. 'Mrs Lookaloft won't squeeze her fine clothes on a bench and talk familiarly about cream and ducklings to good Mrs Greenacre,' he wrote. 'And yet Mrs Lookaloft is no fit companion and never has been the associate of the Thornes and the Grantleys. And if Mrs Lookaloft be admitted within the sanctum of fashionable life, if she be allowed with her three daughters to leap the ha-ha, why not the wives and daughters of other families also?'

It is hard to imagine now, but this was a time when afternoon tea was at the cutting edge of cultural imperialism. Afternoon tea was sexy and fashionable. Henry James came to live in England because he didn't think you could be a proper novelist in America, where afternoon tea was not quite so sexy and fashionable. What could you do, he argued, in a place that had 'No sovereign, no court, no personal loyalty; no aristocracy, no church, no clergy, no army, no diplomatic service, no country gentlemen; no palaces, no castles, nor manors, nor old country houses; no parsonages, nor thatched cottages, nor ivied ruins; no great universities nor public schools – no

Oxford, nor Eton, nor Harrow; no literature, no novels, no museums, no pictures, no political society, no sporting class – no Epsom nor Ascot!'

And what did we have now? We had a royal family that was a joke, and that was falling apart, courted by grinning entertainers and cads, a cowed, barely visible aristocracy, empty pews, vicars who strummed guitars on late-night television, a small, unfashionable army, a creaking heritage industry which could not afford to stem the cracks in our great buildings, a cricket team which was by no means the equal of the teams representing our former colonies, no tennis players who could win any significant competitions, even at Wimbledon, footballers who had not even qualified for the last World Cup, and a racing industry dominated by Arabs. Our motor industry was in the doldrums. Our greatest insurance company, Lloyds of London, was imploding spectacularly. We were a nation known, to ourselves as well as to outsiders, for insularity, ugliness, xenophobia, bad food and bad teeth.

What kind of place was I living in? It was a place of bitterness and envy, a place that had become ashamed of itself, a place where educated people hid their knowledge, where the middle-classes grew up trying to imitate the voices of the poor. We had developed a taste for failure, in the same way that drunks develop an appetite for the self-loathing which drives them to drink even more. We had become known, and knew ourselves, as a nation of losers. We had produced Eddie the Eagle. We had produced Frank Bruno. In Hollywood, our actors portrayed baddies; at home, in soap operas, characters from anything other than poor backgrounds were believable only as villains and rapists. Presenters had been sacked from radio programmes for speaking too properly, on the grounds that they alienated poor people. We were a nation of inverted snobs.

And yet, more shamefully still, we were, even now, instinctively bound by ancient snobberies. We distrusted social mobility. Advancement was a dirty word. Those who had bettered themselves and tried to develop outward signs of this fact were laughed at. When Alan Clark, quoting a colleague, said that Michael Heseltine was 'a man who had bought his own furniture', we knew what he meant. When Robert Kilroy-Silk, the Labour MP who later became a talk-show host, was discovered to have a swimming pool in his back garden, he was taunted and mocked in the tabloids. A swimming pool? Who did he think he was? We despised people who had tried to improve their speaking voices. We still secretly supported some of the values of Nancy Mitford's ideal gentleman, part of whose code of behaviour was to do things slowly, if at all. To hurry was to engage in vulgarity. To have needs was to be common. In the old days, a gentleman would never send a letter by air mail. In 1940, George Orwell said that we were a nation of people with bad teeth who aspired to a state of aristocratic ignorance. We were snobs and we hated snobs. We hated ourselves. We were all mixed up. In 1995, we were presided over by John Major, a man who told us his father had been in the business of selling 'lawn attractions', which were actually garden gnomes, who loved cricket, and who had spent the day before he decided to stand as leader of the Conservative Party at the dentist, having a tooth pulled to facilitate the drainage of an abscess.

* * *

When my cappuccino arrived, I spooned sugar over its chocolatey froth, a habit I had never quite broken. The sugar was white, granulated, pure. It had deep cultural resonance. It was why we'd had an empire in the first place. It was why we'd built plantations on Barbados and Jamaica, and why we got so good at building ships in the 18th century. It was the reason, according to Marx, for the development of the British colonies, the exploitation of which went on to create the conditions for capitalism itself. Sugar was the reason for the West Indian population in London. It was the staple ingredient, the linchpin, of the famously bad British diet. It was, of course, the reason why the molar in the upper left quadrant of my mouth was throbbing, even before it took its first, and last, bite of my lunch.

The sandwich arrived. Floury bread, mayonnaise, salad, soft cheese. I had chosen it partly because it was soft. It had been some time since I'd eaten things that were not soft – French bread, for instance, or toffees, or apples. I picked it up. Fired with the intensity of a man who has just come out of the cinema, I said, 'We can't tell stories about ourselves any more.'

'What?'

'The art of British storytelling has degenerated. We've forgotten how to do it.'

'What are you saying?'

I said, 'We've begun to see ourselves in the third person.'

I'd felt this very strongly. British stories, it seemed to me, were rarely about the people who wrote them. They were about other people. We did not, in other words, write stories about 'us'. We wrote stories about 'them'.

I'd spoken to some writers about this problem. I'd been noticing that, over the last few years, the best British novels had been set outside contemporary Britain. *Money*, by Martin Amis, was set in London and New York, of course, but it was the New York passages which sizzled. Amis's next novel, *London Fields*, was narrated by an American. Ian McEwan's *The Innocent* was set in post-war Berlin. Very atmospheric. Kazuo Ishiguro's *The Remains of the Day* was about people living in a country house in the Thirties. *Possession*, by A.S. Byatt, was set in the past. Pat Barker's *Regeneration Trilogy* was about people going mad in the First World War. *Flaubert's Parrot*, by Julian Barnes, was set in France. The narrator of James Kelman's *How Late it Was, How Late*, which had won the 1994 Booker Prize, was a blind, drunken tramp from Glasgow.

Mark Lawson, who was a Booker Prize judge in 1992, and read 120 contemporary British novels before voting on the shortlist, told me, 'almost no novels were set in contemporary England; if you take "after 1970" to mean contemporary, easily 85 to 90 per cent were set outside of that, frequently in other countries, or in other times'.

I'd talked to Martin Amis. At the time, he was writing *The Information*, a book about two British writers who go to America to promote their books. He sat in an armchair in his flat, contemplating the state of British fiction. He said, 'If you think about what's been the most violent political upheaval in England in the last five years... it has to do with the rates.'

'The poll tax?'

'Yeah. And can you think of a more boring thing? Whereas in America every day you have abortion demos, gay rights demos, police brutality. This is not the rates.'

'Right.'

'Politics is about power,' he said, 'and we haven't got any. We're in the process of divesting ourselves of power.'

Julian Barnes had told me, 'There's no point in doing a little England version of the American novel – the Empire is long dead. What is London the centre of in the world? Symphony orchestras, maybe. Symphony orchestras and royalty. But that doesn't make me want to write a novel about the royal family.'

Bill Buford, who judged the 'Best of Young British Novelists', had said, 'Of the work I read, the very worst was fiction set in contemporary London; it seemed to be a kind of dead zone.'

Having lived in England for most of my life, I moved to London in 1993. Buford was right – in London, you felt as if you were trapped in the ruins of a bygone era. I reviewed films for the *Mail on Sunday*, a conservative mid-market tabloid, and noticed something immediately: Britain was not cinematic. People complained that the British film industry was in trouble because it was underfunded at a government level. But I thought it was in trouble because Britain looked terrible in films. It was as if the camera itself was embarrassed to look at certain things. Panning along a London street, trying to build up a dramatic atmosphere, the camera would seem to get snagged. What did these buildings, and streets, and people, mean? All the images were loaded with tweeness, dullness, class-consciousness. The camera never seemed to arrive at a consensus. As a viewer, you didn't know what you were being told; you just sat there, jittery and bored.

Just about anywhere else was fine. America seemed to have been made for the cinema. When a camera rolled along an American street, the images did create a consensus. They spoke to you with a reassuring voice. You knew you were safe in their hands. American films were happy with their details, their symbols of power and mobility and status. Cars. Guns. Open roads. Skyscrapers. Swimming pools. Prestigious universities. In *When Harry Met Sally*, the recently divorced Harry, played by Billy Crystal, is desolate when somebody mentions the name of a university. Meg Ryan, as Sally, wonders: did his ex-wife attend this university? No, says Harry, 'but they're both Big Ten schools. I got so upset I had to leave the restaurant.' Both Big Ten schools? That's like somebody saying, 'No! She didn't go to Oxford – she went to Cambridge!' This type of line would be more or less impossible in a British film; the very mention of a term such as 'Oxbridge' or 'Redbrick', in a neutral context, would be deeply embarrassing, a signal to be suspicious of the person who uses it. In fact, almost any detail about a middle-class person, or his or her background, schooling, or accommodation, makes us cringe. You can't identify with people who talk like that. Even if one of those people is you.

* * *

I took a sip of cappuccino. The frothy, sugary liquid washed through my mouth and over my throbbing tooth. I slurped, not wanting to create a painful vacuum inside my mouth.

My girlfriend said, 'Don't slurp your coffee.'

I didn't say anything back. I'd mentioned the tooth – my worries about it, the throbbing, the nausea. She had told me to go to the dentist. But I didn't want to go to the dentist. Not quite yet. I wasn't ready for the dentist. In any case, I didn't have a dentist. I'd have to find one. I had a very British relationship with dentists. I didn't see them as hired hands who would do my bidding. To me, dentists were somewhere between policemen and teachers – public servants whose job was to examine, find fault, correct, punish. There is a time when you haven't been to the dentist for a while, and there is a time, not long afterwards, when you know you won't be going back for a while, because you've left it too late.

How had I let my tooth get like this? It had been filled and re-filled, by a succession of dentists – Mr White, Mr Villiers, Mr Day, Mr Archer, Mr Greening. Because of this

35

tooth, I had, over the course of 25 years, waited in a succession of mock-cheerful rooms, with pastel furniture and bright prints on the walls, flipping through copies of the *Daily Mail*, and *Punch*, and *Country Life*, overcome with the specific feeling that is dental dread. Those pangs of anticipation. The need to curb your imagination. Your acute consciousness of details. Your hyper-awareness of the weather outside, whatever it is. It always seems to be drizzling, with a few heartbreaking rays of sun toying with your heart. In a dentist's waiting room, one becomes sentimental. You are struck by powerful waves of nostalgia, even for moments that have only just happened. As the clock ticks down, you are nostalgic for the breakfast you had that morning, for your toaster, for the act of putting on your shoes, for some moments spent waiting at a traffic light. You develop a cultural sweet tooth. Country music makes you tearful. You'd be won over by a Lloyd Webber musical. An early James Stewart film would kill you.

There wasn't much of the actual tooth left. This was my large, central upper molar; the tooth I had used, in childhood, to crunch up gobstoppers and sticks of rock – for years, it had been an anvil hammered with confectionery. At school, I pulverised mint imperials, those creamy pebbles of sugar, with the first bite. I didn't even need to soften them up by sucking them. At that time, I was in a hurry for the sugar rush, and this tooth was my facilitator. I wanted to mainline the sugar, and this tooth acted as my syringe. I knew that its name, molar, was derived from the Latin word *molare*, to grind – literally, to mill. It was first filled in the summer of 1970, and, since then, the milling action had pounded each filling further into the tooth like a wedge, causing cracks, more decay, and the repeated need for a new, deeper filling. In the 1970s, tooth decay worked in tandem with the dental practice of overfilling. My poor tooth had been overfilled. By now, it looked like a cup of greyish tea in a fine porcelain mug.

It was rotten; the enamel on the outside was no more than a façade, a stage-set. Touched in the wrong way, on its chewing surface, it would pang with pain; the heavy, dull stab of nacreous discomfort. This was not the fine, high-pitched pain of recent decay – this was pain felt through rotting tissue, through trapped pus, through sodden, hampered nerves. It was sick-making pain. The pain moved upwards, into the jaw. It had become multi-dimensional. Sometimes it was unbearable. Untouched, the tooth merely throbbed. I'd noticed, that previous winter, that cold air sucked across its surfaces brought, not quite a stab of pain, but a brush with pain, a reminder that pain was there. I'd begun to be careful about my breathing.

The tooth had last been worked on two years earlier. Since then, I'd been uprooted. My life had been through several changes. A relationship had ended; a new one had started. I'd had a buffer period between relationships. I'd moved to London from a town in Sussex, a distance of 50 miles. I'd left my old dental practice behind. Many times I had imagined myself calling a new dentist, hearing the receptionist's bright voice, making an appointment. I imagined a check-up, a dabble with a hygienist, a smiling conversation with the dentist, and no work, or minimal work, needing to be done. But I did not make the call. And after a while, at some point during the buffer period, my tooth had begun to ache.

The buffer period, the time when you do not have a regular girlfriend, but are looking for one, is unhealthy in every sense. All your routines break down. You wake up in unfamiliar beds, hung over, without a toothbrush. To carry a toothbrush in this situation would be seen as presumptuous. And, of course, you don't share a tooth-brush with someone whose bodily fluids you have been warding off with a layer of latex. This is a phase when you worry about the tiny cuts you might have around your fingernails, when you jump from the bed and run to the bathroom, in a semi-crouch, holding your condom which, once the bathroom door is locked, you will inspect for leaks. So sharing a toothbrush is out of the question.

When you are single, and British, you do not, like the Americans, go on organised dates. You just go to social functions, and mill around, and hope to bump into people. You drink more. You never pay your bills. Your exercise and dietary regimes take a hammering, until eventually they atrophy to nothing. Physically, you abuse yourself. You feed on alcohol. You live in a culture of chance meetings, drinks bolted back, conversation which seems witty at the time, but probably is not. Certain faculties – the ability to gauge the sexual attraction another person has for you, for instance – become sharpened. Some things, like going to parties, become prioritised. And other things, like going to the dentist, are shelved.

What happens when you don't clean your teeth? Well, they rot, of course. The mixture of the enzymes in your saliva and the particles of chewed-up food in your mouth turns into a noxious substance which eats away at your enamel. This substance searches out fissures and cracks, particularly around fillings. Teeth rot for the same reasons that buildings rot – liquid, laden with chemicals, permeates the surface, creating bigger holes and abraded areas for yet more liquid to get in. Buildings rot because of water, which is a pity, because cities are usually built on rivers or next to the sea. Teeth rot because of saliva, which is a pity, because they grow in a salivary environment. The mouth is the tooth's enemy.

Of course, you can clean your teeth. Of course you can! You can wake up early in the morning, in a place where you're supposed to be, where you have gathered your tooth-cleaning equipment, with time on your hands, with a positive outlook, without a hangover. When you clean your teeth, you dislodge some of the tooth-rotting fluid from the surfaces of the teeth, and displace it with water. The fluoride in your toothpaste strengthens your enamel. It's a defensive measure, a flak jacket. Day and night, your teeth remain behind enemy lines.

But something happens when you don't clean your teeth – something psychological. You stop worrying about it so much. Not cleaning your teeth, or not cleaning them all the time, becomes a new routine. A wedge is driven into the edifice of your personal responsibility. Also, nothing much appears to be happening to your teeth. Not at first, anyway. As an illness, tooth decay has a long incubation period.

You wake up in an unfamiliar bed, have unfamiliar sex, jump out of the bed, and perform your jinking, crouched run towards the bathroom. You check the condom for leaks. You sit on the edge of the bath, momentarily triumphant, and cast your eyes around the small, damp room, taking in the alien tooth mug, and the toothbrush, which is either multicoloured and pristine, and shaped like a training shoe, or horrid and damaged,

40

like a smashed bird's nest. You survey the bathroom, with its cracked tiles, its damp patches, its awkward plumbing. In London, nobody who will sleep with you at the drop of a hat has a non-decaying bathroom. Soon, you will bolt into the street, having made your vague promises, having not cleaned your teeth, and go to work. The damage to your teeth builds up, undetectable, for months.

My job was to watch films. I watched four, or five, or six films every week. Sometimes I interviewed people. Mostly I sat in small screening rooms with a lot of scruffy old men, some of whom would fall asleep during the film. These were the other film critics. Sometimes there was a snoring crisis – somebody would have to be shaken awake. There were old women, too, and some younger people, like me, who were turning into the scruffy old people who had reviewed films for decades. The critics were the most cynical people you've ever met. They hated nearly everything. They would come out of the films wincing, as if they were actually in pain.

To me, it was the best job in the world. I sat back, numbed by the darkness, the music, the flickering images, while all these stories were pumped into me. As I had come to expect, the British were having trouble with their stories. I already knew we were uncomfortable with ourselves. At best, we made films about the vanished Britain of the past – films like *The Browning Version*,

Mike Figgis's interpretation of a Terence Rattigan play, in which Albert Finney plays a sad old schoolmaster at a public school in about 1950. He is Crocker-Harris, the Latin master, and is universally despised – by the boys, by his wife, played by Greta Scacchi, and even by the headmaster, a smarmy snob played by Michael Gambon. Finney is the last trace of Empire, sadistic but also self-sacrificial, enforcing Latin grammar like a drill sergeant. In the end, we feel uncomfortable. Do we want men like Crocker-Harris to become extinct? When they go, taking their old ideas with them, who will replace them? Who will step into the vacuum?

Outside the comfort-zone of history, the British film-maker had two options. One was the bad-tempered ugly film, which featured people who can't have proper conversations, unattractive public housing, primitive weapons, trainers and aggressive haircuts. Crime is a staple activity. Guns are scarce; people threaten each other at close quarters, with teeth bared. *Shopping*, with its ironic title, is a good example – a film about the British cult of joy-riding and ram-raiding, with Jude Law as a stroppy young outlaw. Here are some of the people who have stepped into the vacuum. This is a film about the underclass – about them, rather than about us. But, even so, the film-makers can't bring themselves to look at these characters too closely; they seem to have no culture or history, no

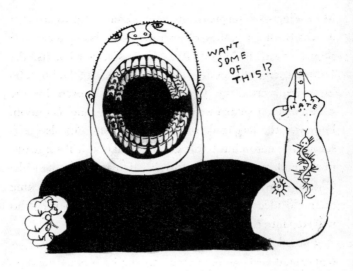

meaningful background, as if they were recent immi-
grants. There it was again – British embarrassment.
British unwillingness to look at the details.

The other option was *Four Weddings and a Funeral*, a
film about bumbling fools who can hardly speak in
coherent English, or do anything much, until a sensible
American puts them straight. *Four Weddings* might
almost be a thesis on how we are ashamed to be middle-
class, and how we are looking for a bigger, better culture
to take us over. It's a British film, but the point of view is
deeply American – that Britain is quaint and silly, a place
where the mannerisms and customs of the people are

being preserved by heritage funding, like an old ruin. I felt I was getting more and more American as the story went on.

Now that the Crocker-Harris generation had disappeared, this was what we were left with in our minds: Jude Law's vacant nihilist and Hugh Grant's cringing fop. Or Alan Rickman and Jeremy Irons, the Hollywood baddies, looking pained and immaculate among the helicopters and explosions, and being stylishly dispatched towards the end by the chunky, quipping hero.

***

A year into the buffer period, I started a new relationship. I moved into the girl's house in Spitalfields, a Dickensian area which was dominated, on the one hand, by curry houses, and the Bangladeshi community which owned the curry houses, and, on the other hand, by the shadow of Jack the Ripper. Jack had killed a prostitute, Annie Chapman, in a house in the street which backed on to ours. As you came and went, you negotiated piles of vomit, always a hazard in a curry zone, and groups of tourists on Ripper tours. I kept a toothbrush in the bathroom. I began to floss, for the first time in two years. But it was too late. At first, the pain in my upper left molar was delicate, almost exquisite, like the pain you feel at the age of six or seven when you tweak a loose baby tooth.

And then I crossed a borderline, and the pain was less delicate. And then it was hardly delicate at all.

The first moment of actual fear, of proper dental dread, came the day I went to see a film called *Deadly Advice*. I stepped out of the house feeling cheerful. There were two piles of vomit on the pavement. Our street ran at right-angles to Brick Lane, which was the main curry strip, and the people who vomited, the City traders and brokers who drank and brayed and lorded it over the Indian waiters, would try to duck into a side street at the crucial moment. Sometimes all they managed was a couple of yards; sometimes they ran down the street a little way. Once in a while, somebody would get as far as our house, eight doors down the street, and there it would be, splashed outside the door like a warning – a congealed reminder of the Raj, of slavery and tiffin, of Kenneth Williams as the Khasi in *Carry On Up the Khyber*.

On this day, the vomiters had not got as far as our house. I took a taxi to Soho, and bought a cup of coffee and a cheese sandwich made with soft white bread.

Deadly Advice is a film set in a small town called Hay-on-Wye, in which Jane Horrocks kills her mother, played by Brenda Fricker, and dumps her in a lake. It looks like it might get interesting until Horrocks starts talking to the ghosts of old Victorian murderers, and the plot spirals out of control. As usual, ordinary, dull, contemporary Britain

45

wasn't good enough. Someone had decided that the story could only be interesting if it had the solid backing of the past, of British murderers from a more stately age, who killed people before the decline set in. Victorian killers! It was a lifeboat to cling to. Even I found myself being vaguely proud of the fact that Jack the Ripper, whoever he was, must have walked past the house I lived in. He had disembowelled Annie Chapman yards away from my tiny back garden. Our house had been a sweatshop full of seamstresses, which, we were told, might have doubled as a brothel. Jack might have been in our bedroom!

In the screening room, trying not to rustle, I took a bite of the soft white bread, and felt my teeth slicing through the cheese in the middle. The pain, and the weird sensation accompanying the pain, came when I started to open my mouth again. Ouch! And what was this? My tooth appeared to be coming out! After the stab of pain, there was a feeling of something being wrenched from its moorings.

I closed my mouth again, and took a swig of coffee, sucking it through my teeth to wash the sticky sludge of bread and cheese away. I opened gingerly, and patrolled my teeth with the tip of my tongue; nothing seemed untoward. I sat there for a while, frightened, as the film lost its direction.

What had happened was this: my filling had been

dislodged. The tooth underneath and around the filling had decayed, giving the lump of amalgam more room; the sludge of cheese, white bread, amylase and saliva had acted like a toffee, like a glue, and stuck it to the surface of the tooth below. Once the glue had gone, though, I could open my mouth at will. By the end of the film, the crisis appeared to be over. The tooth seemed to have settled down; it was not, or not yet, anyway, a volcano on the brink of erupting. It would be fine. I would be careful with it. This was when I began to eat only on the right side of my mouth.

We started looking for somewhere else to live. The attractions of Spitalfields, with its strange shops where you could only buy wholesale, as if you were the proprietor of a curry house, were beginning to pale. Local Bangladeshi residents, genuinely concerned about the tone of the neighbourhood, had been posting threatening letters to my girlfriend. She was a prostitute, they reasoned, because she wore short skirts, and would, if she did not begin to dress more respectably, be among the victims of the forthcoming purge they were planning. 'Go to Hell Hore. Filth Hore, you will Die with all Hores!'

What you do, when you're a middle-class Brit and you want somewhere to live, is look for somewhere old to live. You know, almost instinctively, that you will never be happy living in a new house. What you want is a house with 'character' – literally, a house that has been 'marked', or 'etched', from *character*, the Latin word for an etching tool. We spent a few afternoons every week looking around houses and flats which had been built in the 18th and 19th centuries. In the meantime, we rented a flat above a restaurant in Regent's Park Road. The building was old. We had difficult plumbing, bodged woodwork, an ancient, dusty attic and a faulty boiler; for some time, hot water spurted down the walls of the building, rotting the brickwork at our expense.

Why did we want to live in an old building? Because old buildings had positive associations. New buildings had been built when Britain was declining. New buildings seemed tasteless. New buildings in Britain were not like new buildings elsewhere – Sweden, say, or Switzerland. They were not a continuation of tradition, with balconies and roofs pitched at a charming angle. They were an escape from tradition. By the mid-century, wrote Evelyn Waugh, it had been a typical Englishman's experience 'to be born into one of the most beautiful countries in the world and watch it change year by year into one of the ugliest.' New buildings in Britain were like new towns. They were vulgar. They were experiments that had already failed. They were hutches built during a masochistic, self-flagellating era. Old buildings were falling down, certainly, but at least their bricks had been laid by people who were desperately poor, and frightened of losing their jobs in the cruel Georgian and Victorian economies. New buildings had been built by slackers and yobbos. They were our hairshirt, our sackcloth and ashes, our way of punishing ourselves. No wonder we were having trouble writing about them, and about the people who lived in them. They were stories we didn't want to hear.

All of these things had nagged at me for a while. As a race, we felt both superior and inferior. Both feelings hurt us. We were in a terrible fix. At some point, Britain had lost its mythic allure as a literary landscape. When, if ever, would it come back?

Evelyn Waugh had depicted the seeds of decline in *Brideshead Revisited*, which was published in 1945. Billeted during the war in the crumbling old country seat of his former friend Sebastian Flyte, the narrator, Charles Ryder, is sickened by the fact that one of his fellow officers, Hooper, is not a proper public-school gentleman. Ryder, in a fit of maudlin sentiment and snobbery, thinks, 'These men [Sebastian Flyte's posh relatives] must die to make a world for Hooper... so that things might be safe for the travelling salesman, with his polygonal pince-nez, his fat wet handshake, his grinning dentures.'

Here is Charles Ryder, standing on the edge of a social revolution that would see the rise of commercial values and the collapse of the social edifice so admired by Henry

James. From that moment on, it would be impossible to believe that it was the values of the British class system which ruled the world – no, the power was passing into the hands of men with more practical values, the values of the travelling salesman with the fat wet handshake and the grinning dentures. Of *Brideshead Revisited*, Waugh said that 'he was greatly shaken by its popularity in the USA'.

How much more shaken would he have been, one wonders, had he seen the British television adaptation, filmed nearly four decades after the book was published? In the book, written for a mid-century readership, Waugh depicts Charles Ryder's infatuation with Sebastian Flyte and his family by describing how socially grand they were – they may have lived in a crumbling old house, but this was the very thing that was so great about them. They lived in a house with character. They had the right connections. They knew how to hold a teacup. They symbolised Waugh's values. In the television series, in order to make Ryder's infatuation seem realistic, the part of Brideshead was played by Castle Howard, a vast, pristine palace. Modern viewers wouldn't have understood the idiosyncrasies of Waugh's social values. The director needed the backup of material values to drive home his point. Without Castle Howard to pine for, Jeremy Irons, as Ryder, would have looked like a whimsical nutcase.

And here we were, my girlfriend and I, pining for a crumbling old house we could turn into a palace. We were stuck in the middle, wanting to be posh, ashamed of wanting to be posh, pretending we didn't know if we were posh or not. We loathed Charles Ryder, but we also loathed Hooper. There was very little safe middle ground. We inspected Georgian houses and flats in Islington, Victorian flats in Hampstead and Belsize Park. Edwardian was the limit. I didn't want to live in a house built after my grandparents were born. The prices were outrageous. Some of the plumbing looked medieval. We were fools. We offered money on a flat, three floors of a 170-year-old house in Barnsbury, but it turned out it was unfit for habitation. The interiors were beautiful, but the building was falling down. We viewed a Georgian house in Gibson Square. Feeling faint, my tooth throbbing, I climbed the stairs to the first floor. The front bedroom, right above the entrance, was sloping. It was actually sloping!

'It's sloping,' I said.

'This is what we call Early Movement,' said the estate agent.

***

Not long after that I was sitting in the wholefood café in Soho with the sandwich in my hand, slurping my coffee. I was slurping, rather than sucking, because of my tooth.

'Don't slurp your coffee,' said my girlfriend. I swallowed carefully. I lifted the sandwich to my lips, and slid it into the right side of my mouth, protecting the throbbing left side with my tongue. Gingerly, using my incisors, I nipped off a section of the sandwich, trapping the food momentarily between palate and tongue. A chunk of soft cheese began to slip, unchewed, down my gullet. At this point it was crucial to behave in a counter-instinctive manner. When food is in the mouth of a hungry man, peristalsis begins. The throat sucks. Saliva, loaded with digestive enzymes, spurts from the salivary glands. The teeth begin to chomp. I knew I needed to be careful.

A strip of bread was positioned dangerously between the upper and lower molars on the left side, and... the cheese was blocking my gullet! I began to panic. I breathed through my nose. I could feel the cheese slipping down, slowly, like a sinking ship. Would I choke? Could I choke? Now pure instinct took over; instinct stepped in to save me. There was nothing else for it; I chomped my teeth together. I chewed. For a moment, forced by circumstances, I was gloriously uninhibited. And that was when the tooth went, when it finally snapped.

'Mmm! Mmm! Mmurgh!'

'What?'

'Mmmurgh! Mmm! Mmm!'

'William!'

The fine enamel cup of my tooth had cracked. The pain seared into my jaw. What a surprise! It was a shrieking electrical pulse, a shamefully intimate penetration, a splintering bone-crack, a sharp shredding of nerves, a rending of tissue, a dark welling of liberated pus. An era had ended. A wicket had fallen. The food was stuck; I was, indeed, choking. I could not suck the contents of my mouth down my throat, or spit it out.

I sat, rigid. The pain pulsed through my jaw. I held my breath. It was a cold February lunchtime, the light drizzle punctuated with sporadic sunshine, and I was trying, and failing, to eat a sandwich in the capital city of a country with a serious identity crisis. I was right! It was a nation of lavatorial humour and endemic cynicism, of football hooligans, of beer bellies and white, sagging flesh; a country whose own poor still believed it was the best on earth, which made everybody else aspire to disparage it. I had grown up wanting to disparage it! This was the country that had produced Johnny Rotten, so-called because of his green teeth, and these green teeth had acted like a beacon, leading us into a new era of self-loathing and nihilism. God Save the Queen! No future! Now we were world leaders in degenerate art; a movement whose chief proponent, Damien Hirst, ground his teeth so much he'd had the back ones crowned with gold. We'd lost an empire, and won the war, but facts were beginning to filter out which mitigated our triumph. Vera Lynn had been booked to take part in the 50th anniversary of VE Day. But hadn't Edward VIII, and the Queen Mother, and most of the landowning classes, secretly wanted to side with Hitler? Now the famous 'little boats', which had saved the rump of the British Expeditionary Force after it had retreated to Dunkirk, were mostly hulks, slowly rotting in estuaries and on beaches, while the government was planning to invest money in a new tourist attraction in Greenwich to celebrate the millennium. The white cliffs of Dover were eroding into the sea. We hadn't really won the war. We'd had to rely on the Americans, just as Hugh Grant, bumbling and tongue-tied, had needed to rely on Andie MacDowell in *Four Weddings and a Funeral*. No wonder we had problems telling stories about ourselves.

The pain subsided. It went from mad, electrifying, screaming pain to a new, more active throbbing. I would need painkillers. I slid some of my sandwich to the right side of my mouth. I began the slow process of mastication. Some food had been forced from the back of my throat into my nasal passages. I put the sandwich down. I swallowed.

I said, 'It's my tooth. I think my tooth has cracked.'

My girlfriend said, 'You've got to go to the dentist.'

***

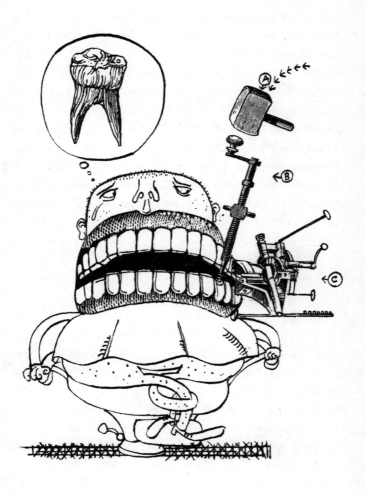

Minutes passed. Days passed. Weeks passed. And here I was, standing outside the surgery, listening for the buzzer, ready to open the door and climb the stairs towards a woman who would, in the next hour or so, say to me, 'Can't you keep still? It's hard enough in the first place, with all this blood', a statement which would make me reel with deathly nausea and self-pity. I had arranged for this appointment. The word, with its dread connotations, rang out through the decades. There was, it turned out, a dental practice a short walk away from the flat we were renting. I'd spoken to a cheerful woman on the telephone. She asked me what the problem was. I told her I thought I might need a filling.

'Have you been experiencing discomfort?'

'Discomfort?'

'Has it been painful?'

'Well...'

What could I say? I didn't want to mention the pain. If I told the truth about the the pain, then they'd realise how bad the tooth was. And if they had an inkling of how bad it was – then what? They'd be... lying in wait. They would be preparing a more serious set of tools. In any case, my tooth had settled down somewhat. If I ate only mushy foods, took painkillers, and tried to forget about it, it was manageable. I could live with it. So I'd told the dental receptionist that I wanted an appointment in a couple of weeks. Two or three weeks. I wanted time to prepare myself.

Also, I had work to do. My tooth an open wound, I watched the best British film of the year, *The Madness of George III*; a story about how, during a politically sensitive period in 1788, George III suffered from porphyria, a disease which makes people rave around, shouting crass and obscene things. It was, at least in part, a skit on the current royal family. It was a film about how Britain was decaying from the top down. The King, played by Nigel Hawthorne, talked to pigs, made funny faces, and spent time trying to break wind. 'Let's try to fart!' he yelled. Later, urinating into a potty, he said, 'Come on, England, come on!'

Edgy about the appointment, I went to interview Martin Amis about his new novel. It was the day before the day before the day itself. Amis had been having dental troubles of his own. His teeth had been denounced in the press. What a coincidence! Perhaps, I thought, I would be able to bond with the author on a dental level. My tooth aching with novel twinges, I walked out into the light drizzle and hailed a taxi. When I arrived at Amis's writing flat, he met me at the door and followed me up the stairs. We sat down. He said he wanted to tell me two things straightaway. He wanted to correct two smears. He pulled out a cigarette paper and loaded it with dark, soggy tobacco. 'I did not abandon my children,' he said. And then he said, 'I did not have cosmetic dentistry.'

He was in a strange position. The son of Sir Kingsley, and the author of several acclaimed novels, he was now less famous than his teeth. Imagine that – you slave for years at your typewriter, you get good reviews, you attain a cult celebrity. You attempt to make good on your early pledge never to write a dull sentence. By and large, you succeed. And then you open a newspaper and discover that you're not as influential as you thought. But your teeth are. Your teeth are getting ahead of you. Your teeth are the story. Poor Martin Amis. One day, he goes to the dentist to get his teeth fixed. It turns out to be a great career move for the teeth. But the novelist gets left behind.

Amis was keen to talk about the teeth. He wanted to reverse the situation, to get back to the good old days, when he was a writer, rather than a controversial dental patient. He took a drag on his cigarette. He said, 'No, this was not cosmetic dentistry. I didn't go to the dentist for cosmetic reasons.'

Here was the nub of the controversy: Amis had paid $20,000 for a course of dental treatment in New York. This was because his teeth were in terrible condition. But people in Britain assumed that Amis was having cosmetic treatment. They wanted to knock him for being vain. So they did. And it worked. It was one of those rumours which stick. For a while you couldn't talk about Martin Amis without people rolling their eyes and talking about his dental vanity. This was the perfect piece of gossip. Who did he think he was – a film star?

He was already courting several other controversies. He'd left his wife, Antonia, for a younger and supposedly more beautiful woman. He'd fired his literary agent Pat Kavanagh, the wife of his friend Julian Barnes. He'd hired a new agent, an American called Andrew Wylie, who is known as 'the Jackal'. He'd dropped his publishing house Jonathan Cape, and moved to the bigger, richer, Murdoch-owned publishing house HarperCollins. He'd asked for, and got, a two-book deal worth £500,000. Who did he think he was – an American?

He'd been overtaken by his teeth, in terms of celebrity, at some point in late 1994. It started when news leaked out about his book advance. The Booker Prize-winning novelist A. S. Byatt accused him of 'male turkey-cocking'. This was a reference to his salesmanship. He'd sold himself for half a million pounds. Byatt said, 'I don't see why I should subsidise his greed, simply because he has a divorce to pay for and has just had all his teeth redone.' Paul Johnson accused him of wanting to 'beautify' his teeth. Stephen Glover wrote, 'We are talking personal vanity and wrong-headedness.' Who did he think he was – Elizabeth Taylor?

Later, Amis would write, 'I was being directed in a film about England.' Here was something very British indeed – a man who had done well was being accused of self-improvement. He hadn't exactly wanted to beautify his teeth – he'd merely wanted to have some teeth so he could eat things properly. But, in contemporary Britain, this was enough to raise a hue and cry, a national wail of self-loathing. A senior British literary novelist, a man who was supposed to be the soul of reticence and self-denial, a man who was expected to be a sort of library-bound, leather-elbowed saint, and who had failed to live up to this stereotype in several ways already, had taken one step too far. He'd gone to an expensive dentist in New York. As a result, something had happened in the home community, something powerful and atavistic, something akin to playground bullying. We had turned on him. Infidel! He was trying to give himself an unfair advantage.

Amis wanted to clear his name. He said, 'The *New York Post* called my dentist. They wanted to talk about my treatment. Mike Szabatura's an ethical chap – he didn't tell them anything. But he told me, he said, "Martin, it doesn't get any less cosmetic than this." '

I sat there, squeezing the side of my molar with my tongue. There was pressure, and more pressure, and then a slow, rasping pang of discomfort. Perhaps I'd need root canal work. Jesus! Amis said, 'I went to the dentist

because there was nowhere else to go. There comes a time when even someone who's become very cowardly and neurotic about facing up to this has to do something. I realised I was absolutely at the end of the rope.' Then he said, 'When my friends say, "Oh, God, I've got some root canal work to do," I just say, "Come on! That's nothing!"'

I climbed back down the stairs. Amis followed, hollow-cheeked, a veteran of the chair. He knew about injections, the slicing of gums, and what he would later call 'sundering'. We shook hands. In the taxi, I wondered how I would feel, 27 hours and 50 minutes later, when I pressed the buzzer.

***

Outside the surgery, the buzzer buzzed. It made me think of the buzz of dental drilling bits, or burs. It reminded me of the deep, almost rattling noise the bur makes when reaming out the inside of a tooth. I stepped inside. Like many British establishments, it was difficult to place in terms of prestige or quality. I was in a Victorian town-house, with steep stairs, distressed old walls, and an aura of gentle decay. Climbing the stairs, I could have been walking towards a professor's classroom or a crack house, a surgery or a massage parlour. At the reception desk, I filled in a form, and made panicky snap judgments based on class-consciousness. White doors, possibly original, with cracked paint; varnished floorboards; a cheerful note on one of the doors, on unpretentious cardboard – 'Waiting Room'. It was not a male-looking place. It looked like an arena of friendly middle-class women, with the possibility of harder, slightly stringy upper-middle-class women lurking somewhere.

Not reassured, I sat on a low sofa. For the moment, I was alone. There were magazines and newspapers. I read about a general who had died, although the obituary did not say what of. He was worse off than me! I looked out of the window at the darkish sky, hoping for a while that my name would not be called. My name was called. Shakily, I walked into the small surgery – a former child's or servant's bedroom, 12 or 13 foot square. There were two women in the room. One was the friendly, middle-class woman I had imagined – the nurse. The other was the slightly stringy, upper-middle-class woman I had feared, a woman with shortish brown hair and a firm, clipped way of saying, 'Okay, if you could just open for me.' Soon, I was lying on my back, looking upwards, gripping the arms of the reclining chair. (The reclining chair! The helplessness of the user of the reclining chair! The way the reclining chair, like Proust's madeleine, opens the sluice gate of memory!) Holding a tiny metal hook, the dentist moved towards my tooth.

***

The earliest memory I have of a dentist moving towards one of my teeth, with the intention of cutting into the tooth, rather than simply poking or prodding it to inspect it, takes me back to 1970. It was the same tooth. It was a hot day. The World Cup was on. A few days earlier, England had lost to West Germany, 3–2, in the quarter-final, a result that had left me desolate. I was to 'have' my first filling, to have part of me removed, drilled away, and replaced by a man-made substance, and I had been banking on England's continued presence in the competition to get me through. Perhaps worse, England were no longer the champions of the world. As far back as I could remember, they always had been, and now that they were not, I felt empty, denuded, unprotected.

I was ten. I'd watched the match with my parents and my younger brother. My parents were mature enough, it seemed to me, to accept the defeat, and my brother, at six, was young enough to deal with this strange new situation, young enough to grow into it. Somehow, though, it came at exactly the wrong time for me. We had scored an early goal, and then a second; destiny beckoned. West Germany, part of a country divided into two halves, essentially because we'd beaten them in the war, which we'd had to do because they'd been mad killers, had pulled a lucky goal back. Then they equalised. It was intolerable. Unable to watch, I left the room and locked myself in the upstairs lavatory. Not knowing what to do, I opened the frosted window and peered out of it over the front lawn. I remember hearing footsteps, my father's, creaking up the stairs. He knocked on the door.

I said, 'They've scored again, haven't they?'

'Yes.'

I experienced the horrible, swirling sensation of blood leaving my face, my stomach dropping, my legs going weak, the sensation you get when, say, you open an envelope and see how much tax you owe, or a printed record of the grades you got. The scorer was Gerd Muller. Gerd the grinder, the molar. I unlocked the door, followed my father down the stairs, and slumped in front of the television, tormented as much by hope as despair, a feeling which would, over the years, become familiar.

Meanwhile, my parents had explained to me about fillings. Part of the tooth had to be drilled away, because it had rotted, because I had eaten so many sweets. At my prep school, where I was a day pupil, we lived in a world of confectionery. In the mornings, we lined up in the local sweetshop and spent as much money as we had in our pockets. The sweets you had were an index of your wealth and influence. Sweets were an early version of other things – clothes, girls, cars, houses. In the dark sweetshop, with its row of glass jars on a shelf high above the counter, I would buy one or two big, flashy items – sherbet dips and quarter-pound bags of dyed, flavoured sugar – and, on top of this, whatever else I could afford, such as the rock-hard balls of cooked sugar called gobstoppers, packets of mints, fruit-flavoured boiled sweets, pastilles coated in granulated sugar, chewy 'gums', or individually-wrapped 'penny chews', which came in fruit or licorice flavours. I favoured the licorice ones, which blackened my tongue and gave my teeth a sinister, rotten look.

At the dentist's, I was told, I would have a choice: I could have an injection in the gum (an injection! In the gum!) or take my chances with the drill. My parents advised the injection, which would be a small amount of pain, but a good investment. I wasn't so sure. Teeth were hard; gums were soft. The idea of something cutting into my gums was hideous. I couldn't imagine what would happen if somebody stuck something into my gums. In any case, they were pink because there was so much blood in them. The sight of my own blood, or even the thought of the sight of it, made me feel ill. In the car on the way to the dentist's, I made up my mind – if at all possible, I would avoid the injection.

Although this would not always be the case, our family used an ordinary, unpretentious dental practice in Lewes. As borderline liberals, my parents were morally opposed to private medicine, but not to private dentistry, which was, in any case, less obtrusive. (Private schools were a different matter.) At this particular practice you could have your dentistry done privately or at the expense of the state; nobody need know. On the way, I was grateful for my mother's careful driving, which postponed our arrival at the place, the dental building, by three or four minutes. At the reception desk, there was some adult talk which went over my head. Then we went into the waiting-room.

What was the quality of my dread, as I sat in the bright, quiet room? Perhaps less than I experience now. After all, nothing worth worrying about had yet happened to me in a dentist's chair. I'd been for 'check-ups', all of which, apart from the last one, I had breezed through. And now I needed 'a small filling' in the large molar in the upper left quadrant of my mouth – my crunching tooth.

A small filling. I expected awkwardness, mild discomfort, the claustrophobic sensation of the dentist towering above me, prodding in my mouth, giving me instructions. I did not expect much else – agony, for instance, or screaming, or blood. I would not have to bleed, would I? Of course not. They knew what they were doing. They would see to it. I was middle-class and British, and, as such, a member of the luckiest race on earth. My mother had told me this. I would, for instance, never have to starve, or be attacked, or contract a dangerous disease. As a nation, we had dealt with all eventualities. We had vaccines. We had discovered penicillin. We had the Domesday Book, and Magna Carta, signed at Runnymede in 1215. We had produced Nelson, Shakespeare, Captain Scott, Concorde. You just had to name it. We had such a well-organised social framework that, uniquely, our policemen didn't even need to carry guns. We were letting black people in, as many as wanted to come, even though we didn't have to. Our borders had been intact for almost a millennium. And if Gordon Banks had been in goal against the Germans, instead of Peter Bonetti, we'd have been in the semi-finals of the World Cup. It was all down to bad luck; it was like King Harold being hit in the eye.

A nurse opened the door every few minutes, and stood in the doorway calling names. As a child, you're always early for dental appointments, and the dentist is always late for them. There is a necessary build-up of tension. When my name was called, my mother led me into the surgery. I was still at the stage of parental supervision at the dentist's. My mother would be there throughout – while I was negotiating about the injection, and after-wards, during the drilling.

The dentist, Mr White, was easy to persuade. Without an injection, he said, the drilling might be 'uncom-fortable.' If it was, though, I could alert him, by raising my hand. If I raised my hand, he would stop drilling. We had discovered a compromise! Mr White tipped me back in the chair, whose leatherette arms I clutched tightly. The nurse slid a suction device under my tongue. And then it was time for the drill.

And here was another thing to be thankful for. When my parents were children, during the war, that great disappeared era of heroism and privation, when the British had their backs against the wall, dental drills had been slow, mechanical grinding devices. By the 1960s, though, high-speed turbine drills had been developed, a technological advance based on Frank Whittle's jet engine. British ingenuity, the envy of the world! The turbine itself, the jet engine which rotated the bur, was in the very tip of the drill. 'The only thing you'll notice,' a friend of my mother's had told me, 'is the smell.'

I said, 'The smell? Why does it smell?'

She paused for a moment, and said, 'Well, it smells because the drill grinds your teeth up into tiny particles.'

My parents and their friends did not, unlike their parents, have bad teeth, or no teeth at all. They had teeth which were declining, but still viable; teeth which would probably see them through. Their dentists had been more primitive, but their food had been less sugary; it was an even trade-off. They were the first generation to trust dentists, to believe that dentists would monitor their teeth on a long-term basis. For my grandparents, dentists were for emergencies only; they lived with the fatalistic understanding that, one day, the emergency would outweigh the benefits of the teeth, which would be pulled, sometimes all at once, under gas. For my grandparents, teeth were things which would turn against them in the end. Teeth were things you had to watch out for. My mother's father, a Newcastle butcher, thought it would be a smart thing to

do to quit while he was ahead. In 1946, at the age of 38, he arranged for a local dentist to etherise him in his front room. When he came round, bleeding profusely, 32 teeth, wiped clean, had been laid out on a white cloth. My grandfather's mouth was full of blood. He never got dentures to fit. It had not been a smart thing to do. In any case, he'd got it over with.

I was told, over and over, that sweet things were bad, and that I should clean my teeth with toothpaste twice a day. Technique was barely discussed. At home, in the mornings, I cleaned my teeth after breakfast; at boarding school, I cleaned my teeth before breakfast, standing at a row of sinks, in double-quick time. I squeezed a blob of toothpaste on the toothbrush, put the brush under a stream of water, and rubbed the minty bristles around my mouth with a frantic, masturbatory action. Sometimes, when food got stuck between my teeth and could not be removed by brushing, I would worry the interdental gap with the end of a compass, trying to hook the particles of bacon rind, or whatever, free from the tender, suppurating spot where they had lodged. Sliding the metal spike between the teeth, and waggling it around, was painful, but in a way which was not unconnected with pleasure. My gums bled, but stopped bleeding quite soon. Once I went too far; once I felt something crack.

I understood the frailties of teeth – how tenuously they

were embedded, how easy it was for them to be knocked out. I had watched from the sidelines, on more than one occasion, as boys were led from the rugby field, teeth having been sheared off at the gum by an opponent's head, the victim's face white, a delta of blood flowing down the chin. Once, at the age of nine, in a flurry of fists, I knocked a boy's front tooth clean out. He staggered backwards, a hand over his wounded mouth; his cry of pain was nasal. It hadn't been my best punch, not by a long way. A glancing knuckle had caught him at the right angle. Decades later, a dentist would tell me that extracting a tooth was one of his easiest jobs. It was a matter of inserting a flat prong, a 'bayonet', and levering the tooth out. 'You just have to get the angle right,' he told me. 'They pop out.'

My father had given me two pieces of dental advice. On the matter of my slightly overcrowded bottom teeth, he told me to refuse any treatment that was offered. 'You'll find yourself looking in the mirror and thinking your teeth have lost their character,' he said. On a more serious note, he told me that one of the worst things one could do to another person was to hold their hands behind their back. This had happened to him as a schoolboy; unable to break his fall, he had fallen on his face, and his front teeth had snapped off. Having his nerves plucked out as part of the subsequent treatment, he described as 'screaming pain'.

Once or twice, when I was scuffling around with friends, he rushed out into the garden, outraged, and said, 'Don't do that! Don't you know the consequences of doing that?' Sometimes my mother would say, 'Have you cleaned your teeth?' When I nodded, she would say, 'Are you sure you've cleaned your teeth?' Mostly, I did. But that was more or less it. I did not floss. I did not massage my gums with the flat sides of interdental 'woodsticks', a practice I later came to believe in. And I ate handfuls of sweets every day.

Mr White moved in. There was a high-pitched noise, and the sensation, not unpleasant, of tiny, cold droplets spraying the roof of my mouth. And the smell. My mother's friend had been right about the smell. There was a moment, very early on, more or less a false alarm, when I raised my hand and Mr White stopped drilling. I was testing the system. And then something appalling happened. Mr White hit a nerve. Pinned down, a white-hot bolt of agony pulsing upwards into my jaw, I was reduced to pure instinct. With no time to semaphore my intentions, I thrashed my head sideways and backwards, a whiplash action of the neck. The drill, still whirring, came to rest momentarily on something much softer than its intended destination – my lower lip. I was rocking forward, screaming, spitting blood, trying to hit Mr White with my balled fists. The whizzing bur had sliced my lip open like a

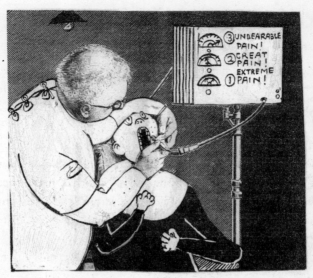

razor blade. Later, when the bleeding had stopped, when the spattered blood had been wiped away, when my loud protests had subsided, when I had stopped sobbing, Mr White persuaded me to have the injection.

***

A quarter of a century later – 24 years and ten months of national decline – I lay back while the upper-middle-class woman dealt with my tooth. Her chairside manner was openly brisk, rather than the usual fawning tone, which is in any case underpinned with briskness. (I once asked a dentist why so many members of his profession committed suicide, and he told me that it was because, in order to make money, dentists must work under severe time constraints; having to make hundreds of decisions, day after day, working in the mouths of panicky people, he said, was extremely stressful.)

The brisk woman filled her syringe behind me, out of sight. Then she was upon me, ready to intrude, to violate. Were some dentists sadists? It was difficult to believe that at least some had not, in one way or another, made their peace with sadism. I was helpless, supine on a custom-made couch, my feet higher than my head, and it all came flooding back to me, the same words, the same process, the same, 'Open wide,' the same, 'A bit wider, please,' the same, 'Wider, please,' the same strained patience, the same, 'Could you keep still for a minute,' and 'Could you just not move,' the same unseen tools moving inside my mouth, the metallic stinging sensation of the needle, always magnified by apprehension, as it penetrates the gum, pumping its mixture of novocaine or lipocaine, to deaden the nerves, and adrenaline, to narrow the blood vessels.

I was lucky; even in my lifetime, dental injections had been significantly less efficient. After the débâcle at the Lewes practice, my mother switched to a slightly more old-fashioned dentist, Mr Villiers of Rottingdean, who operated out of his own house near the seafront. Mr Villiers had been recommended by a friend of my mother's, a slightly go-ahead woman who lived in a house with deep-pile bright orange carpets and black leather furniture. (She was the one who had told me about the smell of drilled teeth.) Mr Villiers, Rottingdean, the Victorian house, the extra cost: it was, dentally speaking, a step up in the world.

But even Mr Villiers's injections were an inexact science. Before being filled, I would be injected, and sent away, back to the waiting-room with its overlapping copies of *Punch* magazine laid out on the coffee-table, to await numbness. Meanwhile, Mr Villiers would be toiling away against the clock, using the valuable 15 minutes to ream out another patient's tooth. (He was, I was told later, a depressive character who drank. Was this true?) I would scan the cartoons, which seemed hopelessly highbrow, and throw myself into the task of appreciating the dry wit of *Punch* columnists such as Basil Boothroyd, who wrote, 'When you hear my new greenhouse is up, you won't be anything like as excited as you would be if it were Enoch Powell's, to take a celebrity at random.' As the numbness spread across my face, I tried to summon up soothing thoughts. The magazines conjured up a Britain that might have existed – a Britain of gentleness, of touching innocence (which must, of course, have been at least partly feigned; imagine calling Enoch Powell a 'celebrity') of fair play, amateurishness, of the sense that civilisation depended, in some way, on comfort, lack of driving ambition, even shabbiness.

My prep school in Brighton bore traces of this sensibility, but it was vanishing fast. In my time, the school itself, a crumbling Victorian edifice, was already condemned; in my last year, we moved into another Victorian building up the road. Brighton, which had always famously contained a mixture of seediness and grandeur, was giving way to true seediness; the lovely squares and sweeping white crescents, once like perfect smiling sets of teeth, were cracking and crumbling, and many of the buildings had been subdivided into apartments and rooming houses. Urban clearance was taking place. There were new tower blocks (which soon looked old), underground car parks, a boxy modern shopping centre. A scrap merchant ran his thriving business a block down from our school, and parked his gilt Rolls-Royce at awkward angles in the clutter of his front courtyard.

Inside the school, some things had not changed for nearly a century. Our blackened wooden desks, with fixed seats and hinged lids, were Victorian, and were inscribed, in some cases, with the penknife-gouged initials of boys who might have died in the trenches of the First World

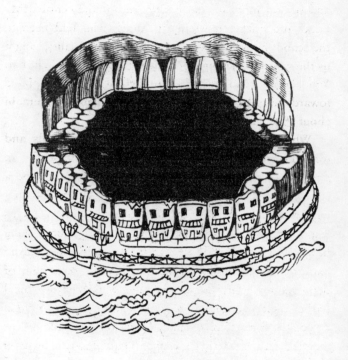

War. There was the 'museum corridor', which contained stuffed animals and birds in glass cases. At least two of my teachers must have been born before Queen Victoria died, and several more in the first decade of the century. My Latin and cricket master, Mr Angel, who had been to the school himself at a time of Edwardian dignity, taught us the value of playing, quite literally, with a straight bat. You had to bend down towards the ball as it whizzed towards you; the advice his cricket coach had given him, in about 1908, had been, 'Smell the ball!'

When we moved to the new premises, pupils and teachers gathered in the school's front courtyard for an opening ceremony, the highlight of which was to be a speech by the England opening batsman Colin Cowdrey, who was, in later years, to become known as 'cricket's last great gentleman'. Cowdrey told us a story about being bowled out for a duck in a Test Match; having walked back to the pavilion, and finding himself in a funk of depression, he left the ground and walked into a local barber's shop to get his hair cut. The barber, watching the match himself on a small television set while he cut people's hair, said to Cowdrey, 'That bloody Cowdrey! Couldn't open a tin of beans!'

Confounded by foreigners, insulted by the working classes, and yet still able to maintain a healthy sense of self-deprecation – this was the peerless Brit, standing on the bridge with a wry smile as the ship went down, shrugging modestly as a hundred prep-school boys applauded.

If the world outside was changing physically, it was also changing spiritually. Perhaps we were the first generation of pupils at the school who were being taught lessons that would not be useful to us; perhaps this was not a rehearsal for life, but a period piece, a series of scenes that we would have to unlearn later in life. Even in 1969, I had an inkling that it would not do to talk posh and make joking use of Latin epithets. I was the boy in the village who went to the fee-paying school, as opposed to the local school, but (and this was a good thing, I feel obliged to say – yes, this was definitely a good thing) the other boys in the village showed not an iota of deference, as they might have in the 1950s. On the contrary, I had to roughen my edges in order to fit in with them. If I was not careful, I would be the one who was written out of the script.

Latin! This was one of the differences between me and the other boys in my village. At my school, Latin was compulsory. 'To learn Latin,' declared Mr Angel, 'is a privilege.' At the age of nine, we declined nouns and conjugated verbs; anybody who raised his hand, at any moment, was offered the opportunity to decline '*bellum*', the Latin word for war, in a single breath. If successful, the pupil in question would be tossed a three-penny piece.

Soon, I was translating simple statements, such as 'The Senate planned to invade Britain', or 'The centurions arrived on the shore'. The Romans who featured in these exercises were pragmatic, imperialistic, and ruthless. What they did was invade and raze places to the ground. I specifically remember the word *vasto* – 'I lay waste.' I learned the word at the age of nine. We had vocabulary tests every week. Learning these words, we were told, would help us with our own language. From *vasto*, for instance, we derived our own word 'devastate'. From '*dens*', the Latin word for tooth, we got dentist, dentition, and also denture. From *carioscus*, the Latin word for crumbling, we got caries.

It seems obvious now, in a way that it did not then, that the British interest in the Romans, which had been revived in the Victorian era, had more to do with our own empire than the Roman one. To the footsoldiers and clerics of the British Empire, schooled in the new public schools of the 19th century, the Romans had a lot to teach us. We studied their culture because it was like ours. We flattered ourselves by learning about Roman military expertise, Roman political cunning. Even in my time, we talked about slavery as a social quirk, rather than a human tragedy of vast proportions. Of course, on one level we must have known that slavery was wrong. But it would have seemed tasteless to argue the point – these were the Romans, and they were fine, inspiring people. In my mind, I could almost picture them moving across the known world, wearing cricket whites and drinking tea.

When I'd arrived at my prep school, in 1969, one warned fellow pupils of the approach of a master by saying 'cave', the Latin word for 'beware'; by the time I left, the tradition had begun to break down. In the early 1970s, we were beginning to want a different sort of relationship with the Romans. One day we were issued with a series of green booklets – the *Cambridge Latin Course*. The booklets, which were illustrated, featured an ordinary Roman family. The father of the family was called Caecilius. They even had a pet. There was a line drawing of a dog, captioned '*Cerberus est canis*'. These people were not senators or centurions. They were humbler, more decent Romans than we had yet encountered. Frankly, they seemed a bit soft. You could not imagine Caecilius raising his voice, let alone razing a city to the ground. In the 1970s British education was already becoming an exercise in the management of shame.

***

'Open wide,' said the stringy upper-middle-class woman. I lay back and parted my lips. She was the eighth or tenth dentist to do this, to take the first, appraising look before getting down to work. After Villiers, my parents had transferred us, as a family, to Mr Day, who removed and replaced Villiers's fillings, just as Villiers had removed and replaced White's. Later, we went to Mr Archer, who removed and replaced Day's fillings, and, later still, to Mr Greening, who flew the flag for preventive dentistry, who was keen on the brushing of the gum margins, who passed us on to a large, fierce female hygienist who made our gums bleed, and who removed and replaced Mr Archer's fillings.

The woman peered into my mouth. My predominant emotions were the ones which had delayed my visit to the dentist in the first place – shame and embarrassment. 'A bit wider, please,' said the woman. Soon she would see my cracked, rotten molar. She would think unpleasant thoughts about me. She would study the build-up of calculus. *Odontia incrustans*. I had suffered *odontoschisis*, the splitting of a tooth, which would necessitate *odontotomy*, the act of cutting into the tooth, in order to facilitate *odontoplerosis*, the filling of the tooth, and, I suspected, *odontotrypy* – the draining of pus from the tooth. The dentist had the syringe in her right hand, thumb on the trigger. She was getting closer, invading my personal space. 'Wider, please,' she said. She slid the needle into my mouth; I could feel the tip of the needle touching my gum, denting its surface, parting the flesh.

Had my education, with its emphasis on stoicism and repression, prepared me for routine traumas like this? Possibly not. At school I'd been beaten, spent two years as an army cadet, and suffered the advances of a master, Mr French, who was a paedophile. I hit him, and, a few days later when I was not expecting it, he hit me back; others were not so lucky. One morning, the school woke to the news that two people were missing – Mr French and an 11-year-old boy. They had disappeared in the night. Days passed with no news. Lessons continued as normal, with speculation discouraged. But some of us, in retrospect, had noticed that Mr French had lately been haunted with a certain desperation. After a week, police discovered the teacher and the boy in a hotel in Torquay. Neither returned to the school, and Mr French was remanded in custody. He was later sentenced to, I think, eight years, for indecent assault. The assaults he had performed on others, including me, had, it turned out, not been indecent – they had been barely decent, but decent none the less.

Once, at the end of a rugby match, Mr French, who had refereed, asked a group of us the question, 'Have any of you got a bag with balls in it?' We were in a bus, waiting to be driven away from the ground. One of the boys said that, yes, he had seen the canvas bag which contained the rugby balls we used to practise with. Bulky, perspiring, with yellowish, oversized incisors, Mr French loomed silently above us, full of unimaginable rage and pain. When, in his annual Speech Day address, the headmaster touched on the subject of Mr French, and the 'regrettable circumstances' in which he had left the school, we shook with barely-suppressed glee, savouring the rich embarrassment of the moment.

Embarrassment! Was this what my life had been about, growing up as a middle-class Brit in the latter half of the 20th century? Sometimes I felt that it was. The embarrassment of one's accent, which had to be carefully modulated to fit in with the accents around you. The embarrassment that you might be too shabby, and the embarrassment, possibly worse, that you might not be shabby enough. The embarrassment that was the result of trying too hard, and being found out; the embarrassment of being nouveau riche; the embarrassment of being seen to improve yourself in any way; the embarrassment of living in a culture that had once, quite recently, been formidable, and finding yourself following the customs of this culture, and thus suggesting, in a host of infinitely subtle ways, that you had not heeded its decline. What was wrong with the British people? Apart from the aristocracy and the lower classes, the people at either end of the scale, the British seemed to have no common ground. They had no consensus or solidarity; they were a group of people split into a million fragments. Some people were trying to cling to the language of Britishness, some to forget it. In my lifetime, the forgetters were edging ahead.

***

In the dental chair, blood pooling gravitationally in my head, I writhed with embarrassment. When the injection took effect, the dentist probed the hulk of my molar with her *patrix*, the male portion of her drill. For the dentist, another etching tool; for my tooth, another character-building moment. I writhed some more. It occurred to me that I was in terrible pain, but unable to apprehend this fact; I didn't have the sense to know it. Very British. My tongue was being pressed downwards. I was in a state of – what was it? Ankyloglossia? I was tongue-tied. I lay there, silent, breathing nasally. That was when the dentist said, 'Can't you keep still? It's hard enough in the first place, with all this blood.' I felt a wave of nausea, a cold, narcoleptic pulse, rolling through my brain tissue. 'Keep absolutely still now,' said the dentist, 'I have to cut through your gum.'

Afterwards, she gave me a prescription for a bottle of antibiotic pills. I'd had an abscess, which had eaten away most of my tooth, and advanced upwards into my jaw. She'd filed the wrecked tooth down to the stump, removed the nerves from the tooth's three roots, packed the root canals with disinfected wadding, and capped the stump

86

with a temporary crown. The abscess, she said, had not definitely been finished off; it was likely to come back, sooner rather than later. She told me to make a second appointment, in the next week or two, so that she could continue the process of disinfection and prepare the root canals for filling. Eventually, a crown would be fitted. I got up out of the chair, made arrangements at the reception desk, and walked back down the stairs, holding my prescription for the pills.

Walking out into the street, I had a Woody Allen moment, the Woody Allen moment I'd looked forward to having all day. In *Hannah and Her Sisters*, Allen, who plays a twitchy, cerebral television producer called Mickey Sachs, goes to see a doctor, terrified that he will find out he is suffering from a brain tumour. When he finds out that he is suffering, not from a brain tumour, but from nothing worse than hypochondria, he leaves the surgery and dances down the street. But his relief turns almost immediately to disappointment. How can he be relieved, or happy at all, when he knows he's going to die?

I did not dance; I took two or three skipping steps. People were around. I was not obviously coming out of a dental surgery. I was coming out of a door between two shop fronts, a door which did not look in any way out of the ordinary. When you are British, you do not dance in the street. You walk formally, with an air of authority, or, failing this, you shuffle along cynically. I shuffled, waiting for the inevitable feeling of disappointment, which, in the blind panic of my pre-dental morning, I had perversely looked forward to. I would feast on disappointment! After all, there was plenty more dental work to do – the filing of my tooth into a stump, the root work, the fitting of the crown. New, more specialist tools would be poked into me with an almost wicked precision – tiny files and 'reamers' to grate the decayed surface of bony matter below the gum line. There would be hours of lying on my back, anaesthetised, tasting blood on the edges of my tongue, hours of trying to keep still and listening, like a tracker in the woods, for tell-tale cracking sounds.

But then a thought occurred to me. Why Woody Allen? Yet again, when I needed a contemporary fictional figure to identify with, my mind had not latched on to a British one. Yet again, my own time and my own place were not good enough for me. I walked on, past the fish and chip shop, past the small supermarket where everything was expensive, past the house where Friedrich Engels had lived when he was helping his strange friend Karl with cash handouts. My trauma was over, for a while at least. Or was it? I'd thought of Woody Allen because the British, unlike the Americans, were finding it hard to tell stories about themselves, and, perhaps because of this, I was having my own creative problems.

I walked up Primrose Hill road towards Hampstead. Here was the very nub of the problem. Personally, I could walk up Primrose Hill Road towards Hampstead without any difficulty. But I couldn't see myself writing about anybody who walks up Primrose Hill Road towards Hampstead. More to the point, I didn't think people would want to read about somebody who walked up Primrose Hill Road towards Hampstead. They'd be asking themselves why this guy was not poor, why he was not a tramp, what he was doing away from the main narrative areas such as the East End. Why was he not in Glasgow? Why not Irish – torn, say, between the IRA and the priests? Why was he not a drug addict or a criminal? Why not gay? Why had he not gone to Africa or India? Why was he not, at the very least, a man in britches from the 18th century?

I was none of these things. I was a middle-class Brit, fairly affluent, heterosexual, ethnically bland. One of my grandfathers had come from Berwick-upon-Tweed. That was the best I could do. When faced with the choice between attending the university of life, and attending an actual university, I had chosen the actual university. As the basis for a fictional character, I was a dead loss.

***

I never bought the pills. I never went back to see the stringy upper-middle-class woman. I decided to stick with what I had – the novelty of a tooth that was not sore, not inflamed, not producing an expanding, molten ball of pus in my jaw. For the moment, I had undergone as much self-improvement as I could take. I had a painless stump. What more did I want? A face-lift? Over the next few weeks, I tried to forget about the tooth. I went on holiday. My girlfriend and I continued to look for somewhere to live. We were looking at stuccoed and redbrick Victorian properties in Belsize Park. The weeks turned into months. We found a flat. We made an offer. The offer was accepted. The stump began to feel tender in what was, at first, not a bothersome way. I turned my attention to other things. I wrote a story about some kids who were very like some kids I had known in my childhood. I changed one character's name from 'Julian Thomas' – the name of the real boy – to 'David Johnson'. A friend who read the story said that these names were so ordinary they seemed obviously made up. I should, he said, use names like Kowalski or Goldberg. Then it would sound realistic. My tooth began to hurt exquisitely.

Another friend told me that he'd chosen his dentist in a novel way: he'd spotted a beautiful girl at a party, and approached her, and suddenly found himself telling her she had beautiful teeth. 'Who's your dentist?' he asked. This was a mixture between a chat-up line and a genuine enquiry – he was himself between dentists, and needed work done; he had spent some years as a heroin user, and had allowed his teeth to go to seed. 'Tim Godzinski,' said the girl. It was the sort of name that I should have used in my story. My friend never saw the girl again, but ended up being treated by the dentist, who was, he said, excellent.

My tooth went downhill suddenly: one day the pain became pressing, then urgent; the next day I was feverish. I woke, sweating and confused, with a strange taste in my mouth, a mixture of sesame oil and soy sauce. Something had burst. My tooth was both more painful and less painful than it had been when I went to sleep. The discomfort was less intense, but somehow more profound. My root canal, I remembered, was full of wadding. Something had clearly been happening to the wadding. The wadding, under bacterial attack, had liquefied, rotted; now it was fully purulent. I found that I could relieve some of the pressure by sucking, hard, on my denuded tooth. There was, it turned out, a hole in the material the dentist had used to temporarily cover the stump. For ten days, I sucked at the hole during the day, and slept fitfully at night.

On the 11th day I found myself supine in a mid-sized room on the second floor of a large townhouse near the Victoria & Albert Museum. My jaw was numb. Sting was emanating from speakers built into the wall. A suction device was vacuuming unwanted fluid and debris from my mouth. Tim Godzinski was leaning over me, turbine in hand, drilling, carefully but firmly, towards the wadding.

I lay, tense, waiting for bad news to be relayed to me, neurologically or otherwise. Godzinski did not know about the wadding. I tried to think of other things. The drill whizzed. I scanned the ceiling, the wall-mounted speakers, the rack of CDs. Sting rang out. Perhaps I would change the name of one of my characters to Godzinski. Yes! On the other hand, this might provide me with new difficulties. Being called Godzinski is the sort of thing that would subtly effect a person's state of mind.

Was I simply the victim of bad timing? Sometimes it felt that way. Born in 1960, I was like somebody running away from a lush, fertile valley, into a desert. The stories were disappearing! Why didn't anybody do anything about it? As I grew up, the small cinemas, where people had queued to see the old-style guys, Jack Hawkins and Laurence Olivier and Noël Coward, and, later, where they went to see Tom Courtenay and Albert Finney and Michael Caine kicking against the old-style guys, were closing down. Multiplexes, which mostly showed non-British films, began to appear. We wanted multiplexes! We'd heard the stories about Britain being great, and we'd heard the stories about Britain being dire, and now that we understood that Britain was dire, it wasn't much of a story any more. The counter-culture, which was kicking authority in the teeth all over the developed world, gave Britain the best kicking of all; Britain, it turned out, had the rottenest teeth.

Godzinski was still drilling. He was hunched. Debris was being sucked away; I could hear the bits as they rattled up the plastic tube. I tensed my neck muscles. I thought about the good British films in my lifetime: *Kes* was about poor people in Barnsley; *Chariots of Fire* was set in the 1920s; *A Bridge Too Far* was about the war; *Ghandi* was about the Raj; *Educating Rita* was about a poor woman embarking on a heartwarming journey, and was, in any case, set in Dublin; *The Draughtsman's Contract* was about ambitious guys in powdered wigs; *My Beautiful Laundrette* was about inner-city Asians; *The Long Good Friday* was about East End crooks.

As I grew up, the rest of us, the ordinary people, were becoming less dramatic and more meaningless – we were, literally, becoming less fabulous, less worthy as subjects for stories. And here's the important thing – we knew it. We could feel it.

Somewhere along the way, recognising the truth of this, British film-makers, like British novelists, had stopped telling stories about people like themselves, and, there-fore, people like me; most of the people I even vaguely recognised in the films I saw and the books I read were foreign. British writers, on the whole, no longer wrote stories about the sort of people who read their books. And what happens to a culture when people don't tell stories about it? It fades away. It disappears from the collective memory.

Of course! It was hard to write about normal people in Britain because normal people in Britain did not know who they were, which was because they never saw themselves reflected in stories. That was why Brits had become too embarrassed and ashamed to say anything about themselves. They suffered from a kind of halitosis of the soul.

Was this my problem? Possibly. For the ordinary, middle-class Brit who wanted to write stories, much of the narrative landscape had rotted away. A story always starts with a crack in the status quo, which is, eventually, mended. But what was the status quo? I had no idea. Where I lived, there was no status quo. My neighbours didn't even talk to each other. If they had, they would have had very little in common. Some drove late-model German sports cars; some drove dented old tubs which had been built before they were born. Some were pretending to be rich; some were pretending not to be rich. Some were pretending to be British; some were pretending not to be British.

I lay there, pinned back, my mouth open, the hinges of my jaw taut, my gums numb, my tongue depressed.

The drill whizzed. I was trapped, boxed-in, mute. To the British writer, it seemed to me, all sorts of places were out of bounds. He was no longer allowed to roam his natural habitat. The British writer was unwelcome in the very places that, according to Henry James, had provided the settings for the whole of English literature. Now there were no gardens, no meadows, no churches, no clergy, no country gentlemen, no palaces, no castles, no manors, no old country houses, no thatched cottages. There were no – what was it? – ivied ruins. There was no Oxbridge. No Eton or Harrow. Certainly no public schools. No received pronunciation. There were things you couldn't say. There were things people didn't want to hear. A veritable halitosis of the soul...

And then – bloop! A mass of something, something dead and rotten, burst upwards from my jaw into my mouth; a lump of it, whatever it was, slurped and slapped its way up the plastic tube. There was that taste again; the powerful mixture of sesame oil and soy sauce, an exaggerated version of the taste you have when you wake up in the middle of the night after you've eaten a Chinese meal. Monosodium glutamate. A yeasty, malty feeling in the mouth. Too tactful to reel backwards in disgust, Godzinski rose and extricated himself from me. He put his drill down, picked up another tool, a hooked needle, and loomed over me again. He poked the new tool deep into the open roots of my tooth. He was looking at something. The wadding! He had found the wadding. Godzinski dipped the needle into the hole in my jaw. Then he removed the needle from my mouth and sniffed at it. Some of the purulent wadding was on the end of the needle. Godzinski offered the needle to his nurse, as if it were a special treat. 'Smell that abscess,' he said.

***

When the wall went, when it finally cracked, we were asleep in bed. We heard nothing. I walked into the garden and saw that the wall had cracked. At first, I thought that the wall had not cracked; the wall could not crack. If the wall had cracked, we would have known about it. There would have been early-warning signs. I must be seeing a crack that was not there. We had just bought a flat; we had just moved in. Flats do not just crack open. But no, the crack was there. It was six foot long, a black fissure in the white stucco. Of course, it didn't matter, because we were insured. I stood in the garden, looking at the crack. I was not unhappy. I was an insured person taking note of an architectural phenomenon. I wondered, as a matter of interest, why the crack had happened. I wondered if it went all the way through the wall.

I called my girlfriend. She came into the garden. The tone of my voice had led her to expect a jovial diversion; a bird or plant doing something. The crack, combined with my tone of voice, alarmed her.

'We're insured,' I said.

The flat had been just what we, as covert heritage snobs, had wanted: the ground floor of a late-Victorian house, with large, high-ceilinged rooms and so on; living there, we had felt, would give us a feeling of belonging. It would give us a sense of identity as Brits. It would recall better times.

The house had been built in 1897 and 1898, during which time Henry James was completing *The Turn of the Screw*, Joseph Conrad was writing *Lord Jim*, Oscar Wilde was working on *The Ballad of Reading Gaol*, Kipling was writing *Stalky & Co.*, George Bernard Shaw was composing *Caesar and Cleopatra*, Max Beerbohm had just taken over from Shaw as the drama critic of the *Saturday Review*, Bertrand Russell was doing early work on *The Principles of Mathematics*, H.G. Wells was bathing in the recent success of *The Invisible Man*, Aubrey Beardsley was dying, and Robert Graves, who lived on the other side of town, was being pushed along in his pram and patted on the head by Swinburne, who, as a baby himself, had been blessed by the poet Walter Savage Landor, who had been patted on the head by Dr Johnson, who, as a scrofulous child, had been taken to see Queen Anne. In a general sense, living in an old house felt better than living in a modern house on a new estate, or a house in one of those closes or squares that was not old, but merely designed to look old.

'You can see right through it,' said my girlfriend, who had walked inside the house, and was looking at me through the crack.

Soon, men would come. Things would be fine. This was when I had a different understanding of insurance. In my mind, insurance was about paying money in case something happened, and then nothing happening. It was a confidence game, based on the fact that you were more frightened of things happening than you needed to be. Still, if a bad thing happened, I believed that men would come, more or less straightaway, to fix it.

My girlfriend was looking at the crack. She looked at me. I was more worried about the effect the crack had on her than the crack itself.

'They'll send someone round,' I said.

We would be back on an even keel, crack-free, in a very short time. This is what I believed. The insurance company would send someone round. As with builders, I visualised ladders, pots of paint, a temporary, jovial rearrangement of furniture, a search for granulated sugar. I visualised an awkward moment or two involving the bathroom, a feigned acceptance, on my part, of offensive opinions. I was ready to field unsavoury remarks about foreigners. I thought of dust, of sheets, of erudite conversations about the general failure of English football at the international level.

A man came. He was brisk and pleasant. He was calm. He wanted coffee with no sugar. I took him into the garden. We looked at the crack. He took notes. To him, the crack was interesting. It was something he wanted to understand.

In the kitchen, he drew diagrams. We talked soil, trees. The crack, formerly so simple, developed complexities. At the time, the man seemed to have exactly the right attitude to the crack; he took it seriously, but had no hint of hysteria.

I went back to see Tim Godzinski. He treated my root canals – washed them, reamed them out, widened them, sluiced them with disinfectant. I paid him as much as I would pay a travel agent for a week in the Caribbean. He spent hours grating their walls, which had become corrupted with pus. The sharp, glinting tools he poked upwards into my jaw looked long enough to snag my eye; I lay there, numb, waiting for a visual disturbance. He filed the hulk of my tooth down to nothing. He filled the roots with molten rubber. He fitted a metal peg into my jaw. He made a cast of my teeth and arranged for a crown to be designed. The crown was an exact copy of my molar. One day, he fitted the crown – the impostor-molar – on to the peg in my jaw. It sat there, a smooth, bulky presence to my tongue, like a modern house in an old terrace. Unfashionable, but practical. Good foundations. Double-glazing. New roof. My dental worries were over.

Time passed. We were in the middle of a beef crisis. In a spectacular act of self-loathing, British farmers had been feeding their animals to each other. The crack in the house got bigger. There were calls and letters. The man who had come and taken notes, it turned out, had been a loss adjuster. Plaster dust seeped from the crack. One night, I found myself alone, frightened, staring at the crack.

Another man came. He was a structural engineer. He wanted tea with no sugar. I walked him into the garden. Again, the crack was approached with stoical calm. In the kitchen, we had a discussion about the crack. The man told us that almost every building in the area had similar cracks. In fact, buildings throughout the city, the whole country even, were developing cracks. They were falling down. It was a bigger problem than people realised.

I said: 'So, when will you be mending the crack?'

My notion, at first, had been that the first man and the second man had come to fix the crack. But I had been wrong; they had come, instead, to report on the crack. They wanted to get the facts about the crack, and give these facts to the insurance company, whose liability was different with different types of cracks. What the crack needed before being mended, the second man told me, was to be 'monitored'.

The monitoring began. A team of men appeared. There was a bucket, a set of heavy tools. The men wore boots. They wanted tea with two sugars. This looked more like it. But the men had not come to mend the crack. They had come to take soil samples. They wanted to study the general terrain that had produced the crack. They dug deep holes, and stuck appliances into the holes. They lay on their stomachs on the ground, peering into the earth. They stayed three days. They took samples of the soil at various depths. They wrapped the samples carefully in plastic sheets. They forgot their bucket.

And then – nothing. *The Full Monty*, a film about a group of unemployed Sheffield steelworkers who make a living as strippers, became the biggest-grossing British film in history. Tony Blair, who smiled a lot, but who had a snaggled set of bottom teeth, was elected as Prime Minister. *Austin Powers*, a spoof about a Bondish secret agent, was a big hit for Mike Myers. Powers, being British, had British teeth – a nice touch. Arundhati Roy won the Booker Prize for *The God of Small Things*, a book about people in India. Diana died. In a German car. A wedge of plaster separated itself from the crack. One day, men came and chopped a tree down in the front garden. There was just a stump. There was talk of tree-root damage, tree reduction. The men were casting around for an easy solution. Somewhere, people were spending time in a laboratory, running tests on our soil, building up information about the crack.

My girlfriend said, 'You said we were insured! You said men would come!'

I said, 'We are insured! It's just that everything is falling down at once! Everything in the country! The insurance companies can't pay out for everything at the same time – they'd go bust!'

Finally, a letter arrived. The crack, it said, was to be mended. That was the good news. On the other hand, there was still some doubt about the way in which it was to be mended, doubt which was not yet resolved. Works were pending, but no date was fixed. It was cheering news. It was better than nothing. Men, I told my girlfriend, would come. They would. It was just a matter of time.

We tried to settle back into our lives. Britain ground on as usual, a mixture of secret pride and showy self-hatred. England were knocked out of the World Cup on penalties. The manager was sacked because he said he believed in reincarnation, and therefore that people who had a bad deal in this life had earned it with bad deeds in the life before. A fine sentiment if you happen to be Asian, but a gaffe for a Brit, who should have known better. The beef crisis deepened. How deep could a beef crisis get?

Concorde crashed. Colin Cowdrey died. Speaking at Cowdrey's memorial service, John Major said, of his life, 'It was a gem of an innings. He lived life with a clear eye, a straight bat and a cover drive from heaven. He was a true Corinthian.' In the same week, 88 per cent of umpires said they thought that cricket had declined, and was now full of cheats. Harold Shipman, a Cheshire doctor, was convicted of poisoning a lot of old and infirm people. The Runnymede Trust, an opinion-forming institution commissioned by the Home Secretary, Jack Straw, declared that the term 'British' was offensive. Later, the Foreign Secretary, Robin Cook, told us that there was no such race as the British. We were disappearing. The BBC spent millions of pounds on a wartime series in which Americans won the war, without our help. Gordon Brown, the Chancellor, had his teeth capped, and became known, for a while, as 'the Grin Doctor'. After Tony Blair made an official visit to the newly-elected George W. Bush, Bush reportedly turned to his aides and said, 'What was that all about?' The Millennium Dome was not a success. In a typically British way, there was too little planning, followed by too much. This is what comes of living on an island; you leave everything to the last moment, because nobody ever invades you. Then you panic. Your enemies, mostly, come from the inside.

And what happened to me? I started to eat French

bread again. I regained dental confidence. I got an electric tooth-brush, designed by a German company, which I kept intending to take out of the box. The men finally came to mend the crack. They drank tea with two sugars. They stripped the plaster off the walls, bonded the old bricks with polyurethane, drove metal pegs into the bricks, and replastered and repainted the walls. Soon after they left, the crack opened up again. I began to write a story about normal, middle-class people like myself. I kept having trouble with the place names. Eventually I abandoned the place names altogether. They were dragging me down. I was also having trouble with the people. There I was, in Hampstead, unable to write the Hampstead novel, or even the Hampstead short story.

One evening, as I was eating some oven chips, I chewed

into a hard one and got a bolt of pain up the side of my mouth. The next morning, I was halfway through an egg-mayonnaise sandwich and it happened again, this time accompanied by a cracking sound. I sat there, unable to swallow, my mouth and throat full of half-chewed gunk which, suddenly, had no immediate destination. It was happening again. This time there had been no warning.

The tooth hurt. Nightmarishly, when I touched it with my tongue, the edge swung outwards, as if it was on a hinge. I kept promising myself I would leave it alone, but a spirit of morbid self-mutilation took over. Each time the tooth swung on the hinge, I got a sharp little pain. I kept swinging the tooth on the hinge. I called Tim Godzinski and made an appointment.

That evening, I was swinging the tooth on the hinge, and there was a clicking noise, and one whole side of the tooth cracked off. Later, I opened my mouth and something big and heavy fell out – the filling that had been in the tooth. It felt like a lump of lead. It was almost a cube, but wider at the top than the bottom. Its size represented hours of drilling, of whizzing and buzzing, of feeling cold droplets of water against the roof of my mouth, of anticipating stabs of pain, sometimes quite reasonably. And then the hole being filled with metal, the squeaking as the metal is tamped down, the taste of the bits of stray metal. Afterwards, the tooth always felt different; it rode a little high in the mouth. Now, it consisted of one sharp fragment and a sinister hole leading into my jaw. I put my tongue a small way into the hole. It felt unreal, infernal, like something from a pornographic dream. This, somehow, was the thing that frightened me most. The hole. What was in the hole? Blood? Bone? Nothing? I did not want to find out.

I sat at my desk and switched on my computer. It was late. My girlfriend came into the room. She said, 'Are you coming to bed?' I told her that I would come to bed later. I had not told her about the tooth. I had not told her about the hole. When she had gone I put my tongue into the hole and pulled it out, quickly. Perhaps, I thought, I should set my story somewhere else. Or I could be unspecific about my setting. That might work. Yes! I stared at the screen. I knew that I would, at some point, put my tongue into the hole again. The screen went blank.

AUTHOR BIOGRAPHY

William Leith lives in London. His teeth are fine, but he will need some crowns doing before long.

Other books in the **FRONTLINES** series:

The Strange World of Thomas Harris
Inside the mind of the creator of Hannibal Lecter
David Sexton

Funeral Wars
How lawyer Willie Gary turned a petty dispute about
coffins into a multi-million-dollar morality play
Jonathan Harr

Last Drink to LA
Cleaning up on the West Coast of America:
confessions of an AA survivor
John Sutherland

Your Pedigree Chum
Like most dog-lovers, Missy's owners think she is irreplaceable –
and they are rich enough to do something about it
James Langton

Nurse Wolf & Dr Sacks
This is New York...a dominatrix and
a doctor share tales of the city
Paul Theroux

Also published by Short Books, **Short Lives:**

The Voice of Victorian Sex: Arthur H. Clough
Rupert Christiansen

The Boy Who Inspired Thomas Mann's
'Death in Venice': Wladyslaw Moes
Gilbert Adair

A Material Girl: Bess of Hardwick
Kate Hubbard

Inventor of the Disposable Culture:
King Camp Gillette
Tim Dowling

Last Action Hero of the British Empire:
Cdr John Kerans
Nigel Farndale

The Hungarian Who Walked to Heaven:
Alexander Csoma de Koros
Edward Fox

Discoverer of the Human Heart: William Harvey
Ronan Bennett

The Hated Wife: Carrie Kipling
Adam Nicolson